T0356287

GENERATION CLAIMED

EMILY ASSELL

WHEREVER YOU ARE

DEVOTIONS AND
DECLARATIONS
FOR MOMS

TYNDALE
MOMENTUM®

A Tyndale nonfiction imprint

Visit Tyndale online at tyndale.com.

Visit Tyndale Momentum online at tyndalemomentum.com.

Visit the author at generationclaimed.com.

Tyndale, Tyndale's quill logo, *Tyndale Momentum,* and the Tyndale Momentum logo are registered trademarks of Tyndale House Ministries. Tyndale Momentum is a nonfiction imprint of Tyndale House Publishers, Carol Stream, Illinois.

Wherever You Are: Devotions and Declarations for Moms

For information about special discounts for bulk purchases, please contact Tyndale House Publishers at csresponse@tyndale.com, or call 1-855-277-9400.

Library of Congress Cataloging-in-Publication Data

A catalog record for this book is available from the Library of Congress.

ISBN 978-1-4964-8863-3

Printed in China

31	30	29	28	27	26	25
7	6	5	4	3	2	1

For the One who has held me, no matter how tired or weak my grip.

And for all those who are weary, but refuse to let go.

CONTENTS

THERE ARE SEASONS IN MOM-ING (AND OTHER AREAS OF LIFE) WHEN TWO MINUTES IS ALL THAT WE HAVE. **BUT JESUS SEES OUR SMALL OFFERING**—OUR FEW MINUTES—AND RECOGNIZES IT FOR WHAT IT IS: ALL THAT WE HAVE, GIVEN TO HIM.

INTRODUCTION

"EMILY, I CAN BARELY TAKE A SHOWER THESE DAYS, much less have time alone with God," my friend Megan admitted as we sat on my back porch, watching our kids run and play. "And when I do, it's only a few minutes, and I just end up playing Bible roulette—quickly flipping through the pages trying to figure out what to read."

"Yes!" my sister-in-law Katie agreed. "And I almost always show up feeling guilty and spend most of my time apologizing to God for not being consistent or not having much time."

This conversation with two close friends hit something deep within me. And the next morning as I pondered it with the Lord, he gave me the idea for this book. Long before the publishers contacted me, proposing a book for moms, I wrote these devotions and declarations for my two sister-friends—and so many like them, daughters whom the heavenly Father longs to draw into his embrace. His heart for them, for you, is why this book exists.

In Luke 21:1-4 (and Mark 12:41-44) Jesus was observing people's offerings at the Temple. There were many wealthy people who put in large amounts. But that is not what impressed Jesus. Instead, he pointed out a poor widow, who gave only two small coins. Jesus recognized her gift for what it was—all that she had. "She gave extravagantly what she

couldn't afford—she gave her all!" (Luke 21:4, MSG). And despite the small amount, he said she had given the most.

There are seasons in mom-ing (and other areas of life) when two minutes is all that we have. But Jesus sees our small offering—our few minutes—and recognizes it for what it is: all that we have, given to him. And, Sister-friend, he is overwhelmed by the amount of our gift.

That is where this book started: the knowledge that our few minutes are precious to God and also that, especially as mamas, our words are powerful. What we say is important. Proverbs 18:21 tells us that the power of life and death are in our tongues, and we will "reap the consequences" of what we say.

Throughout the Bible our faith and our words are linked together. Romans 10:9-10 says that we are saved by believing in our hearts *and* declaring with our mouths. In Matthew 21:21, Jesus says that if we have faith, we can "*say* to this mountain, 'May you be lifted up and thrown into the sea,' and it will happen" (emphasis added). These are just two of the many examples found in Scripture.

You see, our words actually overflow from our hearts (Matthew 12:34). The Father, the Word, and the Spirit cause belief to be born. And if we feed that belief, allow it to grow and fill our hearts, and then let it overflow into what we say, those words have the power to do almost anything. I pray that through this book, you experience the fruit of speaking God's Word out loud over yourself and your family. (More on that in the "Starting Wherever You Are" section.)

I've broken up the hundred devotions into four sections of similar verses. As you read and declare multiple promises and different angles of the same truths, I believe that your heart will be filled and your faith will grow by becoming deeply rooted in his Word. (Another reason for

this approach is that repetition is key in neuroplasticity—aka reprogramming your mind.) At the beginning of each section, I'll also share a little more in depth about how that area has personally impacted my life and can impact yours. The daily devotions are short, meant to take only a few minutes. We will make the most of your precious time with our Father, covering Scripture, words of encouragement, declarations for you and your family, and prompts for praise, thanksgiving, and prayer.

I want to emphasize: *This is not meant to be one more thing added to your to-do list.* Jesus is still calling, "Come to me, all of you [*mothers and daughters*] who are weary and carry heavy burdens, and I will give you rest. Take my yoke [*my way of doing things*] upon you. Let me teach you, because I am humble and gentle at heart, and you will find rest for your souls. For my yoke is easy to bear, and the burden I give you is light" (Matthew 11:28-30). His ways make things easier for us, not harder. He is not requiring us to do or give more (like the wealthy people at the Temple), but instead he wants to transform our little bit to bring life for ourselves, our families, and our world.

Just this morning, my youngest came sleepy-eyed down the stairs. Already feeling behind, I just kept chugging along, trying to fold her into the pace and tasks of the day. But she stubbornly refused—this was *not* our usual routine. "You know I need to start the day with cuddles." So I stopped what I was doing and invited her to come climb up on my lap. We sat in silence for a while as I held her. She slowly melted into me, and I began to whisper into the top of her head how much I love her. Her sweet voice echoed back, "I love you too." Secure in my arms, she talked with me a little more, and then she jumped down and ran off to face the day.

What if we saw our time with our Father the same way? Not as another thing to do, not as penance for failing to show up earlier, not as time to earn or prove love, or to pick up a new fact or technique. But as a moment to pause and be loved.

My prayer is that you view this book as climbing up next to your heavenly Father. May your breath slow as you melt into him. May you hear him whisper his love over you, and may you share a conversation in the security of his adoration and embrace.

STARTING WHEREVER YOU ARE

I WISH WE WERE TOGETHER RIGHT NOW, Sister-friend, and we could laugh and cry and encourage each other on my back porch as our kids run around in the sunshine. But for now, this will do.

I want to start by saying that this book is truly meant to meet you *wherever you are.*

If you are reading this while nursing in your rocker, at the kitchen table with cartoons playing in the background, or on your couch surrounded by a sea of toys and laundry—this book is for you. If you're here and not sure how you feel about God, if you're ready to go all in and declare his promises for your family, or if you're just so tired that you had to read this sentence twice—this book is for you. Wherever you are is right where your heavenly Father wants to spend time with you. And I'm praying his promise that as you seek him, you will find him (Matthew 7:7).

This starting section will take you a little deeper and answer any questions you may have about how the hundred devotions are set up.

SCRIPTURE VERSES

Motherhood seems like the season in which we need God the most but have the least amount of time to spend with him. I know that you don't have an abundance of time to search Scripture for what to read or pray over yourself and your family. So the verses in this book are the ones that have changed me. They are the ones written out and taped to the window over my kitchen sink, saved as my phone's lock screen, and imprinted on my heart. But more than that, I believe they are the ones God chose especially for you. After the main Bible verse is a prompt for a longer passage to read if you have more time. Some of the longer passages are found more than once throughout the book; think of it as a favorite song playing on the radio and believe that the repetition of God's truth is growing your faith.

WORDS OF ENCOURAGEMENT

My words will never be as powerful as the Word, but I hope that sharing some of my thoughts will help grow and change some of yours to match his. May these words encourage you to slow down and see what God wants to speak specifically to you and your heart.

IMPORTANCE OF DECLARING THE WORD

There is power in our words. In James 3:1-6, we are told that our tongues (what we say) are the main mechanism for controlling the direction of our lives. Our tongues are compared to a rudder turning a huge ship in the midst of strong winds and a bridle bit directing the path of a large horse. Even with all the other forces that can affect which way a ship or a horse or a life goes, the ultimate course is determined by the steering device. And we are told that ours is the tongue.

What we say is even more powerful when we use our words to echo God's words. We are told that when his Word is sent out, it will *always* produce fruit, and it will *always* accomplish what God intended it for

(Isaiah 55:11). In Jeremiah 1:9-10, God asks Jeremiah to overthrow some nations and build up others. And how is he to do this? Through God's words: "Look, I have put my words in your mouth!" (verse 9).

Hebrews 4:12 tells us that "the word of God is alive and powerful." We are instructed in Isaiah 62:6-7 to remind the Lord of his promises. Jesus resisted temptation and defeated Satan by quoting Scripture. The Word of God is called "the sword of the Spirit," making it the only weapon of attack in the armor of God (Ephesians 6:17). Again and again, God's will is accomplished by his words being spoken out loud in faith.

I believe you want to speak God's Word and promises over yourself and your family. I believe this because you have bought (and continue to buy) thousands of copies of my book *You Are*—a book that declares Scripture over your children, affirming who God says they are. I have been blessed by stories of you reading this over your children and yourselves, sending it off to college with your older children, using it for Bible studies, and bringing it to the hardest of times and places: psychiatric wards, NICUs, and even grave sites. And those stories always end with our faithful God doing what he said he would do.

Our spoken words overflowing out of the faith in our hearts can produce miracles. Just like Jeremiah, we have things (in our lives and our families' lives) that need to be uprooted, overthrown, and destroyed, and other things that need to be planted and built up. So I encourage you to say these declarations out loud. (Whisper them if you have a little one sleeping.) Because your words, joined with God's, are alive and full of power (Hebrews 4:12).

I have left a blank for you to speak your specific child's name into the declarations. If you have multiple children, please use and adapt the declarations as necessary.

CONNECT WITH YOUR HEAVENLY FATHER

If I'm being honest, it's not always easy for me to come close to God or to perceive him coming close to me. But the Bible gives us a starting place in Psalm 100:4: "Enter his gates with *thanksgiving*; go into his courts with *praise*. Give thanks to him and praise his name" (emphasis added).

After reading each devotion, I invite you to draw near to him by considering two questions based on this Scripture:

1. What is one (or more) thing(s) you're thankful for?

A simple definition for thanksgiving is to express gratitude and celebration for what God has done and provided for you.

2. What is something you appreciate about who God is?

Praise means to appreciate and admire God for his virtues and character.

Set a timer for one minute. Wherever you are, pause and rest in his presence.

I encourage you to set a timer so you won't be anxious about how long this will take (that sounds opposite, right?). Like a party invite without an end time, a lack of clear expectations can cause stress—*Is this going to take up my whole day? How much time do I really have available right now? Have I been here too long or not long enough?* If your timer goes off and you want to stay longer, then of course, feel free to stick around and party all night. But if at the end of a minute, that is all you have to give, know that your heavenly Father is so blessed by the time that you spent with him.

This space is meant for you to take a moment and just be with him wherever you are—physically, spiritually, and emotionally. Take a few deep breaths and lay your head on his shoulder. If you need to be held,

if you need to cry, if you need to be quiet or be loud or anything in between—just *be* with him. Some of my sweetest moments with the Lord have been when I have simply lingered with him and allowed him to love me. Just like cuddling up with my daughter on the couch, words don't always need to be said.

As an aside: This is not meant to be the final word on prayer. As a young mom, talking to God throughout the day was the most effective way for me to pray. I would ask for wisdom, help, or resources as the needs or thoughts came up, following the Bible's encouragement to "pray continually" (1 Thessalonians 5:17, NIV). Think of it as an ongoing conversation that will change and grow as you do. And know that wherever you are and whatever you have to give, your heavenly Father is overjoyed.

HOLDING ON
TO THE GUILT
AND SHAME
DIDN'T KEEP
ME FROM
SINNING—

**IT JUST KEPT
ME FROM
GOD.**

1

FULLY

FORGIVEN

"I'M SORRY. GABE, I'M SO SORRY." I had let my anger get out of control. I yelled rough things at him. I hurt him with my words. His face dropped, and his sister Natalie looked at me with eyes wide and scared. Despite my apology and their quiet murmurs of forgiveness, I felt shame descend on me as my children quickly headed to a different room to avoid being screamed at once more.

I was still in the middle of carrying out a victory over anger. With God's help, I had overcome its stronghold in my life. That didn't mean I never messed up. It meant anger no longer controlled me. But I had to make the decision to use the strategies and truths I had learned. My eruptions were becoming less and less frequent, but I still yelled and failed more than I wanted—especially with the stress of a new baby and minimal sleep.

I repented, but I continued to feel ashamed. I knew better. *Can I really ask forgiveness for the same thing I did last week and might do again tomorrow?* I also worried I was causing more damage to Gabe's heart than just the sad face and broken spirit in the moment. The consequences of my actions were not mine alone to bear.

It wasn't only the anger. There were so many times throughout the day when I did, thought, or said the wrong thing, no matter how hard I tried. I considered myself a complete failure as a mom and couldn't reconcile the words of God's promises with the sin and shortcomings I was still struggling with. *How could I believe I was holy and live in the reality of my failures at the same time?*

• • •

As a child in Sunday school, I loved singing a song based on Titus 3:5. "He [God our Savior] saved us, not because of the righteous things we had done, but because of his mercy." I grew up hearing that we don't earn our salvation. And in school, I had memorized Bible verses about how our faith is what counts as righteousness. But I also knew the verses about how we were supposed to live and act.

All of this led me to inadvertently create my own twisted version of the truth that went like this: I still believed that when I messed up, God forgave me and continued to call me his child. But I also began to suspect that *God was low-key annoyed with me.* That he rolled his eyes (or whatever the divine equivalent would be) when I asked his forgiveness. I imagined a God who was required to forgive me but secretly whispered, "Really? Again?" to his Son, who laid down everything just to see me trip up and stumble repeatedly over the same things. In my mind, God only listened to my prayers, granted me his help, and blessed me when I had sufficiently groveled and apologized for how I had previously wronged him or others.

And even after I had repented, I couldn't be joyful. Surely being penitent and downtrodden for the rest of the day was a much better sign of true repentance than joy. *How could I be joyful when I had caused pain to God and others I loved?*

At night, instead of sleeping, I would review what I had done wrong that day, always vowing to myself and to God to do better. I unconsciously believed that holding on to my shame and punishing myself would keep me from messing up again.

Not surprisingly, this wasn't working well. Who wants to talk to someone they think is disappointed and angry with them? Who wants to dream with someone they believe will remind them of their failures every time they misstep? And *I* definitely didn't want to have my morning coffee with someone I thought required self-abasement before he would extend his love or true forgiveness.

As my relationship with God grew more and more distant, my sin seemed to move closer and closer. *Holding on to the guilt and shame didn't keep me from sinning—it just kept me from God.*

Ironically, the very thing that I thought would condemn me actually freed me. I started reading through the Bible in a different translation that made it harder to skip over verses I had memorized and sang songs about but had not really ever "heard." Jesus is the Word (John 1:1), and he is also the Truth (John 14:6). So the more time I spent with the Word, the more time I spent with the Truth. And that Truth began to set me free (John 8:32).

One of the first passages that caught my heart was Matthew 6:9-13. In these verses, Jesus taught his disciples (and us) how to pray. That prayer, known as the Lord's Prayer, starts with the words "Our Father." Jesus emphasized that before anything else—before we confess our sin, before we praise God's very worthy name, before we call for his Kingdom to come, strategize about our to-do list, or ask for all we need—before all of those important and very good things—he wants us to know him as Father.

Immediately, I thought of my own kids and how my whole being overflowed with joy when I lifted my daughter out of her crib in the morning. I would cover her face with kisses and snuggle her close. And even with my older teenage son, I am thrilled beyond measure when he plops down on the couch next to me. I shoulder up next to him, listening and laughing, encouraging him when needed.

Spending time with my children is a priceless blessing that makes me glad. All my children's failures don't come rushing to mind. I don't require them to apologize or listen to a lecture before I can love them or

listen to their dreams and concerns. Yes, just as a parent wants the best for their child, God knows, addresses, and deals with our shortcomings and failures. He desires that we learn from them and course-correct when needed—for our own good and for the good of his Kingdom, not to satisfy his justice. Jesus already did that.

The more I read, the more my eyes were opened. I cried out with Paul, "I want to do what is right, but I can't. I want to do what is good, but I don't. I don't want to do what is wrong, but I do it anyway" (Romans 7:18-19). But then I continued on to the next chapter: "So now there is no condemnation for those who belong to Christ Jesus" (Romans 8:1).

And in Galatians I read, "When I tried to keep the law, it condemned me. So I died to the law—I stopped trying to meet all its requirements—so that I might live for God" (2:19). Book after book, verse after verse, I heard the same message echoing throughout the entire New Testament.

The truth was that Jesus' blood had already purchased my freedom and my forgiveness (Ephesians 1:7). What pleased God was my faith and my relationship with him, not my perfection. I was wrong about so many things, especially the heart of my Father. So I set out to relearn the truth and then to live it out.

• • •

I remember one of the first times this new understanding was tested. It had been a bit since I had lost my temper, but my patience had been stretched thin during homeschooling that morning. Then later in the day, Gabe and Natalie's playing turned into fighting, and the noise woke up the baby I had just put down for a nap. I erupted with my "scary scream." As my children trudged away, the Holy Spirit quickly convicted me. I repented to God and asked for forgiveness and help to change.

But when I apologized to my children, my son said, "I don't forgive you. I'm still angry at you. You said you were going to try and not yell at us anymore. You lied." I apologized again and explained as best I could that overcoming and changing is a process, not an overnight fix. But he was unmoved. I was heartbroken. My old familiar script rushed to my mind. *He's right. I am a liar and a bad mom. I'll remember this and not do it again.*

As I continued to embrace the pain and punishment of Gabe's words, the Holy Spirit cut in and said, "Who do you believe?"

"But . . . but I hurt him."

"Yes. And God said you were forgiven. Who do you believe?"

Long pause.

The words I had been reading came to mind, and I declared out loud, "I am forgiven by God. It's okay to be upset by the hurt I cause but not to punish myself with it. Jesus' sacrifice does not require my pain or misery in order to make it complete. I can move forward right now in joy and peace. I will not give away the rest of my day to defeat. I am loved, accepted, and holy right now. I choose to believe you."

Gabe did eventually forgive me. And as I continued to defiantly reject condemnation and shame, I saw an unexpected result: The mercy I accepted from God began to more easily overflow out of me to my children and family. I was slower to anger and quicker to listen and forgive. God, the Word, and the Spirit changed me by changing the way that I thought (Romans 12:2).

All our striving and self-shaming cannot bring us victory. I love how Romans 8:3-4 reads in *The Message*:

> God went for the jugular when he sent his own Son. He didn't deal with the problem as something remote and unimportant. In his Son, Jesus, he personally took on the human condition, entered the disordered mess of struggling humanity in order to set it right once and for all. . . . The law always ended up being used as a Band-Aid on sin instead of a deep healing of it. And now what the law code asked for but we couldn't deliver is accomplished as we, instead of redoubling our own efforts, simply embrace what the Spirit is doing in us.

I don't mean that we should ignore the Holy Spirit's call to freedom or his power that allows us to overcome. But don't misunderstand what Jesus died to give you. When he cried out from the cross, "It is finished!" (John 19:30) and gave up his spirit, Jesus "finished" all the requirements for your salvation and for your identity as God's child.

Father God, as we spend time with you and your Word, transform the way we think. May your Word find good soil in our hearts and minds. May your truth multiply and produce a large harvest in our lives and in the lives of those we love. Thank you, Jesus, for making us holy. Thank you for your sacrifice that allows us to come boldly before the Father's throne. In the precious name of Jesus, we pray all of this. Amen.

WHY STAY CHAINED TO WHAT GOD HAS ALREADY BROKEN?

1

YOU ARE . . .
FREE FROM SHAME

So now there is no condemnation for those who

belong to Christ Jesus. And because you belong

to him, the power of the life-giving Spirit has freed

you from the power of sin that leads to death.

ROMANS 8:1-2

(If you have more time: Romans 8:1-15.)

Mama, you don't have to be controlled or manipulated by the bullies of sin and shame. They will guilt and blackmail you into giving up your freedom. But through Jesus, God liberated us from sin's control and rescued us from its consequences of death. Why stay chained to what God has already broken? You are free. So refuse to listen to the voice of condemnation any longer. Remind yourself that you are accepted by your Father and freed by the power of the Spirit.

DECLARE OUT LOUD OVER YOURSELF

I live by the power of the life-giving Spirit and am no longer manipulated by sin and shame. They have no authority over me.

DECLARE OUT LOUD OVER YOUR CHILD

[Child's name] lives by the power of the life-giving Spirit and is no longer manipulated by sin and shame. They have no authority over [name].

CONNECT WITH YOUR HEAVENLY FATHER

What is one (or more) thing(s) you're thankful for? What is something you appreciate about who God is? Set a timer for one minute. Wherever you are, pause and rest in his presence.

2

YOU ARE . . .
PARDONED

He has removed our sins

as far from us as the east is from the west.

PSALM 103:12

(If you have more time: Psalm 103:1-22.)

Let go of your guilt. Holding on to what God has released will not help you. Punishing yourself with the memory won't make you less likely to repeat the offense or more deserving of forgiveness. Jesus has already paid for your wrongs. We don't need to add anything to make the sacrifice complete. We can accept his forgiveness and start over *right now*. Don't wait until you think you have suffered, mourned, or repented enough. God has already removed your sins from you. It was his joy to do it.

DECLARE OUT LOUD OVER YOURSELF

My sins are removed. I will not hold on to what God has released.

DECLARE OUT LOUD OVER YOUR CHILD

[Child's name]'s sins are removed. We will not hold on to what God has released.

CONNECT WITH YOUR HEAVENLY FATHER

What is one (or more) thing(s) you're thankful for? What is something you appreciate about who God is? Set a timer for one minute. Wherever you are, pause and rest in his presence.

3

YOU ARE . . .
RIGHTEOUS

For Christ has already accomplished the
purpose for which the law was given. As a result,
all who believe in him are made right with God.

ROMANS 10:4

(If you have more time: Romans 9:30–10:4.)

Mama, shout "Hallelujah!" Jesus Christ has already accomplished the purpose of the law on our behalf. He met all the requirements and avoided all the temptations. He did all the work, and you don't have to add anything else. Your failures and shortcomings cannot take away what Jesus already did. Only he could achieve God's goal, not us. But we *do* get to share in his victory celebration and prize. You are righteous—right now. You are accepted—right now. You are holy—right now. Jesus took on and completed the job for us all.

DECLARE OUT LOUD OVER YOURSELF

Glory to Jesus who has made me righteous and welcomed me before the throne of God.

DECLARE OUT LOUD OVER YOUR CHILD

Glory to Jesus who has made [child's name] righteous and welcomed them before the throne of God.

CONNECT WITH YOUR HEAVENLY FATHER

What is one (or more) thing(s) you're thankful for? What is something you appreciate about who God is? Set a timer for one minute. Wherever you are, pause and rest in his presence.

4

YOU ARE . . .
FAULTLESS

Even before he made the world,

God loved us and chose us in Christ

to be holy and without fault in his eyes.

EPHESIANS 1:4

(If you have more time: Ephesians 1:3-11.)

Precious Daughter, due to Jesus you are without fault before God. He made a way for us to be holy so that he could make a way for us to be his daughters. Your Father loved you and chose you before the world was even created. He decided to make you holy not based on your own perfection or what you could do for him but because he loved you. From the very beginning, God's plan didn't rest on you or your actions, but on Jesus.

DECLARE OUT LOUD OVER YOURSELF

Because I was chosen and loved by God before the world was even created, he sent Jesus to make me holy and faultless.

DECLARE OUT LOUD OVER YOUR CHILD

Because [child's name] was chosen and loved by God before the world was even created, he sent Jesus to make them holy and faultless.

CONNECT WITH YOUR HEAVENLY FATHER

What is one (or more) thing(s) you're thankful for? What is something you appreciate about who God is? Set a timer for one minute. Wherever you are, pause and rest in his presence.

5

YOU ARE . . .
SET RIGHT

We know very well that we are not set right with God by
rule-keeping but only through personal faith in Jesus Christ.
How do we know? We tried it—and we had the best system
of rules the world has ever seen! Convinced that no human
being can please God by self-improvement, we believed in
Jesus as the Messiah so that we might be set right before
God by trusting in the Messiah, not by trying to be good.

GALATIANS 2:16, MSG

(If you have more time: Galatians 2:16-21.)

Sister-friend, you are accepted and on good terms with God—right now. It doesn't matter if you get the laundry done today, lose your temper with your kids, or let them watch too much TV. Neither your failures nor your accomplishments have any effect on God's approval of you. He is not waiting for you to "do better" before he considers you right with him. Choose, right now, to live with the faith that you are righteous because you have loved and accepted his Son.

DECLARE OUT LOUD OVER YOURSELF

No matter what I do or don't do today, I am accepted by God because of Jesus Christ.

DECLARE OUT LOUD OVER YOUR CHILD

No matter what [child's name] does or doesn't do today, they are accepted by God because of Jesus Christ.

CONNECT WITH YOUR HEAVENLY FATHER

What is one (or more) thing(s) you're thankful for? What is something you appreciate about who God is? Set a timer for one minute. Wherever you are, pause and rest in his presence.

We believed in Jesus as the Messiah so that we might be set right before God by trusting in the Messiah, not by trying to be good.

GALATIANS 2:16, MSG

6

YOU ARE . . .
WELCOMED IN

Let us go right into the presence of God with sincere hearts fully trusting him. For our guilty consciences have been sprinkled with Christ's blood to make us clean, and our bodies have been washed with pure water.

HEBREWS 10:22

(If you have more time: Hebrews 10:11-23.)

Dearest Daughter, your heavenly Father does not want you to wait to come to him until you have it all together or have made yourself as worthy as you can. He sent Jesus to make you clean and pure so that right now you are accepted and welcome in God's presence. Even with your shortcomings and messiness, he sees you as his daughter, beautiful and holy. You can fully trust his heart for you.

DECLARE OUT LOUD OVER YOURSELF

I come into God's presence, clean and loved.

DECLARE OUT LOUD OVER YOUR CHILD

[Child's name] comes into God's presence, clean and loved.

CONNECT WITH YOUR HEAVENLY FATHER

What is one (or more) thing(s) you're thankful for? What is something you appreciate about who God is? Set a timer for one minute. Wherever you are, pause and rest in his presence.

7

YOU ARE . . .
HELPED

Let us [with privilege] approach the throne of grace [that

is, the throne of God's gracious favor] with confidence *and*

without fear, so that we may receive mercy [for our failures]

and find [His amazing] grace to help in time of need

[an appropriate blessing, coming just at the right moment].

HEBREWS 4:16, AMP

(If you have more time: Hebrews 4:14–5:3.)

God welcomes us to come before his throne with our heads held up, not dragged down by guilt. When we enter his presence, we do so as beloved and blameless daughters. Because of Christ, we don't need to fear being shunned or shamed. He gives us his mercy for our failures and his assistance when we need it most. So we can approach the throne as his children, confident of our Father's favor and desire to help.

DECLARE OUT LOUD OVER YOURSELF

God desires to give me his mercy, his help, and his grace.

DECLARE OUT LOUD OVER YOUR CHILD

God desires to give [child's name] his mercy, his help, and his grace.

CONNECT WITH YOUR HEAVENLY FATHER

What is one (or more) thing(s) you're thankful for? What is something you appreciate about who God is? Set a timer for one minute. Wherever you are, pause and rest in his presence.

8

YOU ARE . . .
PURSUED BY HIS LOVE

Surely your goodness and unfailing love

will pursue me all the days of my life, and I will

live in the house of the LORD forever.

PSALM 23:6

(If you have more time: Psalm 23:1-6.)

Precious Daughter, there is nothing you can do to lose God's love and nowhere you can go where his love will not follow. Again and again, throughout God's Word, we see his children struggle, fail, and go the wrong way. And again and again, we see a God who goes after them, redeems them, and uses them even when they fail. His goodness and love will never stop coming for you and your family. He will not give up on you. He will continue to pursue us—his children—until the end of our days.

DECLARE OUT LOUD OVER YOURSELF

God's goodness and love will never quit coming for me.

DECLARE OUT LOUD OVER YOUR CHILD

God's goodness and love will never quit coming for [child's name].

CONNECT WITH YOUR HEAVENLY FATHER

What is one (or more) thing(s) you're thankful for? What is something you appreciate about who God is? Set a timer for one minute. Wherever you are, pause and rest in his presence.

9

YOU ARE . . . CHANGED

I will give you a new heart, and I will put a new spirit in you. I will take out your stony, stubborn heart and give you a tender, responsive heart.

EZEKIEL 36:26

(If you have more time: Ezekiel 36:25-38.)

Multiple times throughout his Word, God promises to give us new hearts and new spirits. Don't believe the lie that you haven't been changed and still have a sinful, stubborn, hard heart. Yes, sometimes you may feel that way, but your feelings are not always truth. Declare and believe that your spirit is tender and responsive to him and his Spirit. You are a daughter made new and have been gifted a heart that responds to and embraces your Father and his ways.

DECLARE OUT LOUD OVER YOURSELF

I have a new heart and a new spirit. My heart is not stubborn or stony; it is tender and responsive to my Father.

DECLARE OUT LOUD OVER YOUR CHILD

[Child's name] has a new heart and a new spirit. [Name]'s heart is not stubborn or stony; it is tender and responsive to their Father.

CONNECT WITH YOUR HEAVENLY FATHER

What is one (or more) thing(s) you're thankful for? What is something you appreciate about who God is? Set a timer for one minute. Wherever you are, pause and rest in his presence.

10

YOU ARE . . .
BEING TRANSFORMED

When God is personally present, a living Spirit, that old,

constricting legislation is recognized as obsolete.

We're free of it! All of us! Nothing between us and God,

our faces shining with the brightness of his face.

And so we are transfigured much like the Messiah,

our lives gradually becoming brighter and more beautiful

as God enters our lives and we become like him.

2 CORINTHIANS 3:17-18, MSG

(If you have more time: 2 Corinthians 3:7-18.)

Mama, we have been given the incredible hope that God can transform us. We are free to be who he says we are instead of stuck with how we have always been. This transformation comes when we focus on following his Spirit's guidance, instead of meeting the expectations of others. When we are before God face-to-face, with nothing between us, we cannot help but be changed by him and reflect his glory to our family and this world.

DECLARE OUT LOUD OVER YOURSELF

I am being transformed to reflect more and more of God's glory.

DECLARE OUT LOUD OVER YOUR CHILD

[Child's name] is being transformed to reflect more and more of God's glory.

CONNECT WITH YOUR HEAVENLY FATHER

What is one (or more) thing(s) you're thankful for? What is something you appreciate about who God is? Set a timer for one minute. Wherever you are, pause and rest in his presence.

GOD LOVES YOU TOO MUCH TO LEAVE YOU WHERE HE FOUND YOU.

11

YOU ARE . . .
BEING MADE PURE

If we confess our sins, he is faithful and just

and will forgive us our sins and purify us

from all unrighteousness.

1 JOHN 1:9, NIV
(If you have more time: 1 John 1:1-10.)

Daughter, God does not just forgive you and then walk off. When you accept you are wrong and admit your sin to him, he commits to the process of removing it from your heart and life. He responds to your desperation and need with his divine Word and Spirit. They come alongside us, working with us to remove the rot, heal the wound, and encourage new growth. God loves you too much to leave you where he found you. He is faithful to draw out our impurities—not to condemn us, but to free us.

DECLARE OUT LOUD OVER YOURSELF

God is removing all the unrighteousness from me and purifying me.

DECLARE OUT LOUD OVER YOUR CHILD

God is removing all the unrighteousness from [child's name] and purifying them.

CONNECT WITH YOUR HEAVENLY FATHER

What is one (or more) thing(s) you're thankful for? What is something you appreciate about who God is? Set a timer for one minute. Wherever you are, pause and rest in his presence.

12

YOU ARE . . .
GOING TO MAKE IT

Therefore, since we are surrounded by such a huge crowd of

witnesses to the life of faith, let us strip off every weight that

slows us down, especially the sin that so easily trips us up.

And let us run with endurance the race God has set before us.

We do this by keeping our eyes on Jesus, the champion

who initiates and perfects our faith. Because of the joy

awaiting him, he endured the cross, disregarding its shame.

Now he is seated in the place of honor beside God's throne.

HEBREWS 12:1-2

(If you have more time: Hebrews 12:1-13.)

God acknowledges that this road is long and—at times—strenuous. So he calls us to drop everything that will make our journey harder and strip down to only what's essential. There are farther places he wants to take you and higher mountains for you to climb. Lock your eyes on Jesus, who considered shame to be an unworthy foe, not even deserving of his energy or attention. Let his example fuel your endurance, urging you forward, and directing you toward the joy of the finish line and his waiting arms.

DECLARE OUT LOUD OVER YOURSELF

I strip off the weight of sin and shame, and I joyfully run with endurance to finish the race God has set before me.

DECLARE OUT LOUD OVER YOUR CHILD

With God, I strip the weight of sin and shame off [child's name] so that they will joyfully run with endurance to finish the race God has set before them.

CONNECT WITH YOUR HEAVENLY FATHER

What is one (or more) thing(s) you're thankful for? What is something you appreciate about who God is? Set a timer for one minute. Wherever you are, pause and rest in his presence.

13

YOU ARE . . .
FORGIVEN

You have come to Jesus, the one who mediates

the new covenant between God and people,

and to the sprinkled blood, which speaks

of forgiveness instead of crying out for

vengeance like the blood of Abel.

HEBREWS 12:24

(If you have more time: Hebrews 12:18-24.)

Because of Jesus, there is immediate and complete forgiveness. Your heavenly Father is not holding anything against you. When you sin, he doesn't remember all the other times he has had to forgive you and get annoyed. The debt for everything you have done in the past and will do in the future has already been paid in full, his sacrifice planned since before the world began. Jesus' blood forever satisfied the need for justice. Pause and receive it, Mama.

DECLARE OUT LOUD OVER YOURSELF

Jesus' blood continues to echo forgiveness throughout my life, forever silencing the voice of vengeance.

DECLARE OUT LOUD OVER YOUR CHILD

Jesus' blood continues to echo forgiveness throughout [child's name]'s life, forever silencing the voice of vengeance.

CONNECT WITH YOUR HEAVENLY FATHER

What is one (or more) thing(s) you're thankful for? What is something you appreciate about who God is? Set a timer for one minute. Wherever you are, pause and rest in his presence.

14

YOU ARE . . .
GIVEN GRACE

The LORD longs to be gracious to you;

therefore he will rise up to show you compassion.

For the LORD is a God of justice.

Blessed are all who wait for him!

ISAIAH 30:18, NIV

(If you have more time: Isaiah 30:18-30.)

Dearest Daughter, do you know what the Lord longs for when he thinks of you? God's words are not, "I long to change her" or "I long for her to get it together." No. He says, "I long to be gracious to her. I want to give her good things, to empower and equip her." He doesn't jump up to scold or yell at you. He gets up from his throne so he can come close to you and offer his love and compassion. We can have the faith to patiently wait on him because we know he only wants good things for us.

DECLARE OUT LOUD OVER YOURSELF

The Lord desires to show me grace and compassion.

DECLARE OUT LOUD OVER YOUR CHILD

The Lord desires to show [child's name] grace and compassion.

CONNECT WITH YOUR HEAVENLY FATHER

What is one (or more) thing(s) you're thankful for? What is something you appreciate about who God is? Set a timer for one minute. Wherever you are, pause and rest in his presence.

15

YOU ARE . . . COMFORTED

Sing for joy, O heavens! Rejoice, O earth!

Burst into song, O mountains! For the Lord has

comforted his people and will have compassion

on them in their suffering.

ISAIAH 49:13

(If you have more time: Isaiah 49:13-23.)

Oh, Mama, let his arms wrap around you now. He is tender when you are hurting. He does not desire to see you in pain. When you are broken, he will not loudly remind you of your mistakes or what you did to deserve this. Your suffering is not a tool to him. There is gentleness and compassion in his eyes. He will not abandon you in your grief. Relax in his arms as he draws you near to comfort you with his presence.

DECLARE OUT LOUD OVER YOURSELF

God is compassionate to me; I am being comforted by him.

DECLARE OUT LOUD OVER YOUR CHILD

God is compassionate to [child's name]; they are being comforted by him.

CONNECT WITH YOUR HEAVENLY FATHER

What is one (or more) thing(s) you're thankful for? What is something you appreciate about who God is? Set a timer for one minute. Wherever you are, pause and rest in his presence.

God is compassionate to me;
I am being comforted by him.

16

YOU ARE . . .
ADVOCATED FOR

My dear children, I am writing this to you so that

you will not sin. But if anyone does sin, we have an

advocate who pleads our case before the Father.

He is Jesus Christ, the one who is truly righteous.

1 JOHN 2:1

(If you have more time: 1 John 2:1-6.)

Sometimes, even after we repent, we can still feel as though Jesus is upset and will reject us until we have paid our penance or proved we won't make the same mistake again. But, Sister-friend, that is a lie. The beautiful truth is that Jesus welcomes you with open arms and stands beside you before the Father. He defends you and supports you. He upholds you when you are weak. Jesus reminds God (even though God already knows) that you are his child and are righteous because of his sacrifice on the cross. Jesus is not your accuser; he is your big brother who backs you before all of heaven.

DECLARE OUT LOUD OVER YOURSELF

Jesus has not rejected me in my sin; he pleads my righteousness before God and all of heaven.

DECLARE OUT LOUD OVER YOUR CHILD

Jesus has not rejected [child's name] in their sin; he pleads their righteousness before God and all of heaven.

CONNECT WITH YOUR HEAVENLY FATHER

What is one (or more) thing(s) you're thankful for? What is something you appreciate about who God is? Set a timer for one minute. Wherever you are, pause and rest in his presence.

17

YOU ARE . . .
PATIENTLY LOVED

Yahweh! The LORD!

The God of compassion and mercy!

I am slow to anger and filled with

unfailing love and faithfulness.

EXODUS 34:6

(If you have more time: Exodus 34:5-11.)

Sister-friend, it is important to the Lord for you to know that he is slow to get angry with you but always full of love and faithfulness. He specifically describes himself this way to reassure you that he is not impatient or easily annoyed with you. You don't have to mentally cower before him, dreading the moment he will bring up all your wrongs or snap at you in frustration because you blew it again. No, God reveals himself as overflowing with love and faithfulness. He wants you to know that his heart is full of compassion and mercy for you.

DECLARE OUT LOUD OVER YOURSELF

The Lord is patient and loving with me.

DECLARE OUT LOUD OVER YOUR CHILD

The Lord is patient and loving with [child's name].

CONNECT WITH YOUR HEAVENLY FATHER

What is one (or more) thing(s) you're thankful for? What is something you appreciate about who God is? Set a timer for one minute. Wherever you are, pause and rest in his presence.

18

YOU ARE . . .
UNDERSTOOD

We do not have a High Priest who is unable to
sympathize *and* understand our weaknesses *and*
temptations, but One who has been tempted
[knowing exactly how it feels to be human] in every
respect as *we are, yet* without [committing any] sin.

HEBREWS 4:15, AMP

(If you have more time: Hebrews 4:6-16.)

From his throne in the heavens, Jesus came down to earth. He became human and vulnerable to pain and hunger and weariness. He worked through messy relationships, struggled with the expectations of others, and had the needs of so many resting on his shoulders. At times, he had to get away from it all too. He even needed naps. When you whisper, "I'm so tired . . . I just want to give up . . ." or "This really hurts," feel his arms around you. Listen as he whispers to you, "I know, Daughter. I know. It's okay. I've got you. You are held. You are understood. You are loved. I am here."

DECLARE OUT LOUD OVER YOURSELF

I am understood by the One who gave up everything for me.

DECLARE OUT LOUD OVER YOUR CHILD

[Child's name] is understood by the One who gave up everything for them.

CONNECT WITH YOUR HEAVENLY FATHER

What is one (or more) thing(s) you're thankful for? What is something you appreciate about who God is? Set a timer for one minute. Wherever you are, pause and rest in his presence.

19

YOU ARE . . .
GIVEN COMPASSION

As a father has compassion on his children,

so the LORD has compassion on those who fear

him; for he knows how we are formed,

he remembers that we are dust.

PSALM 103:13-14, NIV

(If you have more time: Psalm 103:7-18.)

Mama, when we see our little ones struggling with something that is beyond their ability or knowledge, our hearts are overwhelmed with compassion for them. Getting close and crouching down, we do our best to soothe their frustration and encourage them to keep trying, giving advice and help if needed. Our heavenly Father does the same for us. He is not demanding or demeaning; he is gentle and encouraging. He knows and understands all your strengths and all your weaknesses, all your limitations and all your capabilities. He created you just the way you are and bends down to help when you call to him.

DECLARE OUT LOUD OVER YOURSELF

The Lord knows my limitations. He has compassion for me.

DECLARE OUT LOUD OVER YOUR CHILD

The Lord knows [child's name]'s limitations. He has compassion for them.

CONNECT WITH YOUR HEAVENLY FATHER

What is one (or more) thing(s) you're thankful for? What is something you appreciate about who God is? Set a timer for one minute. Wherever you are, pause and rest in his presence.

20

YOU ARE . . . CLEARED

I will be merciful toward their iniquities,

and I will remember their sins no more.

HEBREWS 8:12, ESV

(If you have more time: Hebrews 8:6-13.)

Jesus' sacrifice brought about a new reality. Our sins are not held against us. They are cleared, wiped out, erased. God does not reference a divine tally full of red marks when we ask for help or come into his presence. He is merciful toward us. Our shortcomings are forgiven and then forgotten. We don't have to tiptoe around him, hoping we don't retrigger his simmering anger. We can trust his forgiveness and not linger on what he has already forgotten. We get to restart right now.

DECLARE OUT LOUD OVER YOURSELF

I trust that God has forgiven and forgotten my sins.

DECLARE OUT LOUD OVER YOUR CHILD

I trust that God has forgiven and forgotten [child's name]'s sins.

CONNECT WITH YOUR HEAVENLY FATHER

What is one (or more) thing(s) you're thankful for? What is something you appreciate about who God is? Set a timer for one minute. Wherever you are, pause and rest in his presence.

YOU ARE A BELOVED DAUGHTER OF THE KING OF KINGS. YOU DO NOT BOW TO SIN OR LIVE IN FEAR ANY LONGER.

21

YOU ARE . . .
NOT A SLAVE

You have not received a spirit that makes you
fearful slaves. Instead, you received God's Spirit
when he adopted you as his own children.
Now we call him, "Abba, Father."

ROMANS 8:15

(If you have more time: Romans 8:1-15.)

Precious Daughter, God wants you to be free, not chained to a new master to be afraid of. Jesus didn't die so your deed of slavery would be transferred over to his Father. No, his sacrifice made us free children of God. His desire was for us to live in and be transformed by his love and abundance, not to continue in constant fear of not being or doing enough. Our relationship with him means that we don't have to worry about ruining everything with one misstep or mistake. You are a beloved daughter of the King of kings; you do not bow to sin or live in fear any longer.

DECLARE OUT LOUD OVER YOURSELF

My chains of slavery have been destroyed. I live free and loved as a daughter of God.

DECLARE OUT LOUD OVER YOUR CHILD

[Child's name]'s chains of slavery have been destroyed. They live free and loved as a child of God.

CONNECT WITH YOUR HEAVENLY FATHER

What is one (or more) thing(s) you're thankful for? What is something you appreciate about who God is? Set a timer for one minute. Wherever you are, pause and rest in his presence.

22

YOU ARE . . .
FREE

Christ has set us free to live a free life.

So take your stand!

Never again let anyone put

a harness of slavery on you.

GALATIANS 5:1, MSG

(If you have more time: Galatians 5:1-18.)

Daughter, you are a slave no more—not to any substance, food, illness, mindset, fear, shame, judgment, person, or any other created thing or being. Freedom is not something you have to earn. It has already been purchased for you. Now begins the work of believing it with your actions. Lift your head. Take your stand. Claim what is yours. Ask the Spirit for guidance and help. And refuse to settle for less than everything that has been purchased for you.

DECLARE OUT LOUD OVER YOURSELF

I am free.

DECLARE OUT LOUD OVER YOUR CHILD

[Child's name] is free.

CONNECT WITH YOUR HEAVENLY FATHER

What is one (or more) thing(s) you're thankful for? What is something you appreciate about who God is? Set a timer for one minute. Wherever you are, pause and rest in his presence.

23

YOU ARE . . . RESTORED

Since we've compiled this long and sorry record

as sinners . . . and proved that we are utterly

incapable of living the glorious lives God wills for us,

God did it for us. Out of sheer generosity he put us

in right standing with himself. A pure gift.

He got us out of the mess we're in and restored

us to where he always wanted us to be.

And he did it by means of Jesus Christ.

ROMANS 3:23-24, MSG

(If you have more time: Romans 3:19-28.)

Sister-friend, on your own, you are utterly incapable of living the glorious life God wants for you. We feel this deep in our beings. Some days seem to shout it right in our faces. But instead of letting those days pull us down, let them trigger within us a response of praise. Thank God he has rescued and restored us to be with him. And because of Jesus, we can receive blessings and benefits we didn't earn on our own but that come through his sacrifice and the Spirit's enablement within us.

DECLARE OUT LOUD OVER YOURSELF

God has forgiven and restored me.

DECLARE OUT LOUD OVER YOUR CHILD

God has forgiven and restored [child's name].

CONNECT WITH YOUR HEAVENLY FATHER

What is one (or more) thing(s) you're thankful for? What is something you appreciate about who God is? Set a timer for one minute. Wherever you are, pause and rest in his presence.

24

YOU ARE . . .
REFRESHED

Now repent of your sins and turn to God, so
that your sins may be wiped away. Then times
of refreshment will come from the presence
of the Lord, and he will again send you Jesus,
your appointed Messiah.

ACTS 3:19-20

(If you have more time: Acts 3:12-26.)

Daughter, our Father longs to free you from your sins. When you come to him and repent, his forgiveness will lift off the heavy burden of guilt and shame. It's like when your baby carrier is removed after a long walk and the breeze blows across the damp place where it had been sitting. There is relief and sweet refreshment when the weight is taken off and fresh air can reach that area again. Drop the weariness of your sin, and he will bring you rest and peace, rejuvenating you with his presence and Spirit.

DECLARE OUT LOUD OVER YOURSELF

My sins are gone. My slate is wiped clean. His presence is refreshing me.

DECLARE OUT LOUD OVER YOUR CHILD

[Child's name]'s sins are gone. Their slate is wiped clean. His presence is refreshing them.

CONNECT WITH YOUR HEAVENLY FATHER

What is one (or more) thing(s) you're thankful for? What is something you appreciate about who God is? Set a timer for one minute. Wherever you are, pause and rest in his presence.

25

YOU ARE . . .
NOT GOING TO FALL

Now all glory to God, who is able to

keep you from falling away and will bring you

with great joy into his glorious presence

without a single fault.

JUDE 1:24

(If you have more time: Jude 1:17-25.)

Oh, Daughter, he is, after all, our Savior—the One who saves. He will hold you tightly so you don't fall away. Your salvation doesn't depend on your strength or reasoning. God will never force you to stay or take away the free choice he has given to all humanity. But when we cling to him, he will never let us go. Because of Christ, we are faultless before God. Not even our own sin can separate us from him. He welcomes us into his presence with exuberant joy.

DECLARE OUT LOUD OVER YOURSELF

God will not let me fall away; I stand faultless before him.

DECLARE OUT LOUD OVER YOUR CHILD

God will not let [child's name] fall away; they stand faultless before him.

CONNECT WITH YOUR HEAVENLY FATHER

What is one (or more) thing(s) you're thankful for? What is something you appreciate about who God is? Set a timer for one minute. Wherever you are, pause and rest in his presence.

2

INCOMPARABLY

LOVED

"GOD, WHY DID YOU MAKE ME THIS WAY? Why couldn't you have made me _____?" And then I would fill in the blank with whatever my current obsession was at the time: taller, thinner, smarter, funnier, etc. Comparison and insecurity were not things I consciously thought about, but they were definitely my norm.

That messed-up mindset had squatted comfortably in my life when I was younger—take a look back at the late 90s and early 2000s for a cringeworthy refresher on what was being paraded around. A trip to the mall and our local Abercrombie & Fitch would have me rethinking how I felt about myself for days after. But none of those things were what God used to get my attention and free me from this way of thinking.

Oh no, it was much later with the new girl at church when my true state was finally brought front and center. Now looking back, I can see how God was using this situation; but back then, I believed that all my jealousy was justified, and all my insecurities were her fault. My pettiness was on full display.

"She got invited shopping, and I didn't. . . . Of course she's tiny; she hasn't had any babies yet. . . . She just gets all the attention because she's new. . . . She's not really crying; it's all an act. . . . She doesn't need help; she just needs attention. . . . Why can't anyone see how manipulative she is? . . ." And on and on it went. (In case you're wondering, we're close friends now, and she proudly allowed me to share this story as a testimony of God's redeeming power in our lives. In fact, you'll find her in the intro as part of the inspiration for this book.)

Once jealousy starts burning strong, it spreads. A different girl at church was put in charge of all the party and potluck planning, and I had a hissy fit. My poor husband, Matt, had to hear me go on and on about how no one was recognizing my enthusiastic worship, my loud "amens," or any of my other standout achievements that made it obvious I was meant for more than just bringing the fruit platter.

True, I could barely organize my own shopping list and dinner plan for our family, but I could excel at anything if someone would just call out my potential and give me loads of attention and mentoring time. Also, I didn't particularly enjoy planning or figuring out details or being behind the scenes. But still, I was offended.

There was always someone causing me to be jealous and petty. Whether online or in person, so many women just wanted to show off how much better they were than me. This couldn't be me or my problem. I was sure everyone else was to blame.

So what finally happened? I eventually got miserable enough and convicted enough to know I needed to change. The Holy Spirit faithfully reminded me of Romans 12:2, "Let God transform you into a new person by changing the way you think."

Recognizing his leading, I brought all my feelings to God and dug into his Word. I wrote Bible verses about comparison on a stack of note cards. Then whenever my mind (or mouth) started wandering down that path, I stopped what I was doing and read them out loud. I began to pray and confess that I believed his Word over my feelings, and that I humbly needed his Spirit's help to change.

• • •

The end of the Gospel of John is a bit different. Matthew, Mark, and Luke all end with the story of either Jesus being resurrected or ascending, but with the same message: encouraging us to go and tell and make disciples. But the last story John tells does not follow the pattern.

Following his resurrection, Jesus appears to his disciples along the

Sea of Galilee and prepares them breakfast. Afterward, with Peter's earlier three-part denial hanging between them, Jesus intentionally creates this very personal, marked moment in Peter's life by asking him three times, "Do you love me?" He singles Peter out and redeems his failure. Jesus then goes on to prophecy about Peter's future and finishes with an encouragement: "Follow me" (John 21:19). After this amazing one-on-one experience with Jesus, what does Peter do? He turns around, sees John, and asks Jesus, "What about him?" (John 21:21).

Goodness gracious, can I relate to Peter! How about you? God has singled us out, gone to great lengths to redeem our stories, and given us a beautiful plan for our lives. He charges us, just as he did Peter, "Follow me." And we are so encouraged and steadfast . . . *until*. Until we look around and say, "What about her? What about her family? Or her calling? Or her home?" And you know what Jesus says to Peter and to us?

"What is that to you? As for you, follow me" (John 21:22). What does it matter what John or your sister or the new girl at church is doing? Does that change what God has planned for you? Does that change what you're supposed to do? No.

My husband calls it "putting on blinders." Growing up in the rural Midwest, we used blinders to restrict a horse's vision. The device goes on either side of the eyes to block out distractions behind and next to the animal and help them focus on the race or job right in front of them. In addition, many horses spook easily and can hurt themselves or others when overreacting to a perceived threat; blinders keep them safer and calmer. I love this visual image, and I started picturing myself putting on blinders in situations where I felt the need to compare and compete.

Still, when I found myself on the winning end of the comparison game, I had a much harder time not wanting to play it. In fact, many times I purposely compared myself to people I thought I was superior to. "Wow! That mom's kids don't listen at all." Or how about, "If I were her husband, I wouldn't put up with that," or "Can you believe she wore that?" But whether I lost or won, whether I was offended or offending, God saw I was still struggling in this area, and he wasn't done with me yet. He continued bringing me to freedom with these verses:

> The very credentials these people are waving around as something special, I'm tearing up and throwing out with the trash—along with everything else I used to take credit for. And why? Because of Christ. Yes, all the things I once thought were so important are gone from my life. Compared to the high privilege of knowing Christ Jesus as my Master, firsthand, everything I once thought I had going for me is insignificant— dog dung. I've dumped it all in the trash so that I could embrace Christ and be embraced by him.
>
> PHILIPPIANS 3:7-9, MSG

The Holy Spirit seemed to be shouting the last part: "I've dumped it *all* in the trash so that I could embrace Christ and be [*fully*] embraced by him" (verse 9, emphasis added). With my spiritual eyes, I saw myself standing face-to-face with Jesus. My arms were full of "all the things" I thought were important enough to hold on to: my popularity, others' opinions, feeling superior, jealousy, unforgiveness, and more. His arms were extended, inviting me to him.

I put down some of the big things I was holding, but I still clung tightly to a few favorite ones, things like unforgiveness and worrying about other people's opinions. But keeping even just one of them was like trying to figure out how to hug someone with a baby in your arms or a toddler on your hip. *Maybe I can do a one-arm side hug or try to just lean in, gently protecting the small bundle I have between us. . . .*

I paused.

I looked at Jesus and his outstretched arms.

Then I whispered, "I choose you." I bent down and placed it *all* on the ground. I stood up with my arms completely empty and ran straight into his waiting ones. "Nothing compares to you. I don't want anything that keeps me from you. I choose to fully embrace and be fully embraced by you."

Time and time again, Sister-friends, I have found myself in front of Jesus, being invited into his arms. I have knelt down to release things and gotten back up with skinned knees and tears streaming down my face. But you know what? Nothing has ever compared to his embrace. It doesn't feel like giving up or losing or sacrificing when at the end I get him.

● ● ●

I was thankful the Lord freed me from comparison, but I hadn't dealt with my inner feelings and beliefs about myself. I was constantly trying out a new lifestyle hack, workout habit, or hairstyle. Deep down, my core belief was that I didn't measure up. I remember repeating the lie, "I am not enough and too much all at the same time." God had begun to transform me, but he wanted me *fully* free.

When he called me to write my first children's book, *You Are,* it felt like a recap of all he had been teaching me, especially regarding the power of our words and his Word. Every night when my husband was at work, I would put our three kids to bed and then write. This meant

that multiple times a week, I was spending hours searching and lingering in God's Word. I researched, meditated, and prayed through what God wanted his children to know regarding who they were and what he thought of them.

Almost without realizing it, those verses became my vocabulary and how I spoke to my three children. I became more intentional about speaking words of life *out loud* instead of just keeping those thoughts and words to myself. When an encouraging or grateful thought came to mind, I said it.

"Natalie, that was so sweet. You have such a beautiful heart."

"Gabe, God has such a big plan for your life, and I'm so happy I get to watch it happen."

"Thank you, Jesus, for this sunshiny day."

And then one Mother's Day, something different happened. I was pumping gas, savoring a moment of quiet outside while my kids were all buckled safely in their seats—Mamas, I know you get me—and I caught a glimpse of my own reflection in the car window. Without thinking, I quietly whispered into the eyes of the girl looking back at me, "I love you."

The surprise of it stopped me hard. My eyes got watery, and a lump formed in my throat. God had been true to his Word. Sometime during those quiet, intimate nights, he had transformed my mind. And as his Word sunk down deep, my heart—despite knowing its flaws and mistakes—began to believe it too. It wasn't about looks or sizes or performance. I am loved and lovable because of who I am: God's daughter.

Mama, the same is true for you. You are loved and lovable because you are his daughter. He doesn't see you as a project or a means to an end. You are more to him than anything you do for him. He designed

every intricate part of your body, your mind, and your personality. And he delights in every bit of you (Psalm 139)!

If the God of the universe, who speaks only truth, delights in you, maybe you can believe that you are delightful. And very possibly, you could be delighted with yourself too.

Father God, may your love permeate our hearts, souls, and bodies. We take up your Word, the sword of the Spirit, and with it we destroy every false stronghold that has been set up in our minds about who we are and how you feel about us. Holy Spirit, show us what needs to be laid down so we may fully embrace and be embraced by our Savior. Thank you for the assurance of your love. We choose you. We love you. We are your daughters. In Jesus' high and holy name, we pray all these things. Amen.

26

YOU ARE . . .
DEARLY LOVED

A voice from heaven said, "This is my dearly
loved Son, who brings me great joy."

MATTHEW 3:17

(If you have more time: Matthew 3:16-17; 17:1-5.)

Twice God spoke these words audibly about his Son, Jesus. He didn't say, "Because . . ." He didn't say, "When . . ." He didn't list Jesus' deeds or characteristics. He said, "He is my Son. He is loved. He brings me so much joy." God says the same about us countless times throughout his Word. Pause and take a deep breath. Shut out whatever is going on within and around you. And hear God's gentle whisper: "You are my dearly loved daughter. You bring me so much joy."

DECLARE OUT LOUD OVER YOURSELF

I am God's dearly loved daughter. I bring him joy simply because I am his.

DECLARE OUT LOUD OVER YOUR CHILD

[Child's name] is God's dearly loved child. [Name] brings him joy simply because they are his.

CONNECT WITH YOUR HEAVENLY FATHER

What is one (or more) thing(s) you're thankful for? What is something you appreciate about who God is? Set a timer for one minute. Wherever you are, pause and rest in his presence.

You are my
dearly loved daughter.
You bring me so much joy.

27

YOU ARE . . .
A DELIGHT

The LORD's delight is in those who fear him,

those who put their hope in his unfailing love.

PSALM 147:11

(If you have more time: Psalm 147:1-11.)

Daughter, you delight God Most High—not because you are perfect, not because of any task you have done or sin you have defeated. He smiles because you put your hope in his love. Trusting God is one of the highest compliments you can give him. He counts your faith as worship. When you honor and respect him as your Father and your God, his heart is overjoyed. We hope and trust in our Father's unconditional love for us, not in anything we have done or will do.

DECLARE OUT LOUD OVER YOURSELF

My hope is in my heavenly Father's love, and he delights in me.

DECLARE OUT LOUD OVER YOUR CHILD

[Child's name]'s hope is in their heavenly Father's love, and he delights in them.

CONNECT WITH YOUR HEAVENLY FATHER

What is one (or more) thing(s) you're thankful for? What is something you appreciate about who God is? Set a timer for one minute. Wherever you are, pause and rest in his presence.

28

YOU ARE . . .
CAUSE FOR REJOICING

The Lord your God is in the midst of you,

a Mighty One, a Savior [Who saves]! He will

rejoice over you with joy; He will rest [in silent

satisfaction] *and* in His love He will be silent *and*

make no mention [of past sins, or even recall

them]; He will exult over you with singing.

ZEPHANIAH 3:17, AMPC

(If you have more time: Zephaniah 3.11-20.)

Our Mighty God delights in *you*. In his love, he does not bring up all the ways you have failed or remind you of what has happened in the past. He is quiet about your sin and loud about his delight in you. Your Father sings you a love song. Just as we find such joy and awe in our own children, your Father feels the same when he looks at you. You bring a smile to his face and gladness to his heart. He does not look at you with criticism but with eyes full of love.

DECLARE OUT LOUD OVER YOURSELF

The Lord is so delighted by me that it causes him to sing and shout!

DECLARE OUT LOUD OVER YOUR CHILD

The Lord is so delighted by [child's name] that it causes him to sing and shout!

CONNECT WITH YOUR HEAVENLY FATHER

What is one (or more) thing(s) you're thankful for? What is something you appreciate about who God is? Set a timer for one minute. Wherever you are, pause and rest in his presence.

29

YOU ARE . . . SEEN

Thereafter, Hagar used another name to refer to the LORD, who had spoken to her. She said, "You are the God who sees me" [in Hebrew: *El Roi*]. She also said, "Have I truly seen the One who sees me?"

GENESIS 16:13

(If you have more time: Genesis 16:1-16.)

El Roi: The God who sees me. The name was given to God by a desperate, overwhelmed mother—a mom who thought no one understood, no one saw what she was going through or how much she had already given. To an imperfect, rejected, weary mother, God shared a part of himself that no one else recorded in Scripture had yet experienced. And he saw her as no one else in this world could. He is the God who sees you and shares himself with you in return. Pause right now and be seen. Pause right now and see him.

DECLARE OUT LOUD OVER YOURSELF

I am seen by my God, and he allows me to know him as well.

DECLARE OUT LOUD OVER YOUR CHILD

[Child's name] is seen by God, and he allows them to know him as well.

CONNECT WITH YOUR HEAVENLY FATHER

What is one (or more) thing(s) you're thankful for? What is something you appreciate about who God is? Set a timer for one minute. Wherever you are, pause and rest in his presence.

30

YOU ARE . . . MORE THAN WHAT EVERYONE ELSE SEES

The LORD said to Samuel, "Do not look at his appearance or his stature. . . . Man does not see what the LORD sees, for man sees what is visible, but the LORD sees the heart."

1 SAMUEL 16:7, HCSB

(If you have more time: 1 Samuel 16:1-13.)

Daughter of the Most High, God sees your heart—not the dishes still in the sink, the dry shampoo in your hair, or the snot running down your child's face. Let's defiantly refuse to worry about how the world sees us or our littles because that's not what God sees. When he looks at your child, he bypasses the temper tantrums, the stained outfits, and all the knots you hope stay hidden inside your little's ponytail, to see their *heart*—a heart that is learning and trying and sometimes failing. And God sees your heart, too, Sister-friend. He knows your desires, recognizes your best intentions, and rejoices in all your efforts for him and your children.

DECLARE OUT LOUD OVER YOURSELF

The Lord looks past what others see and sees my heart.

DECLARE OUT LOUD OVER YOUR CHILD

The Lord looks past what others see and sees [child's name]'s heart.

CONNECT WITH YOUR HEAVENLY FATHER

What is one (or more) thing(s) you're thankful for? What is something you appreciate about who God is? Set a timer for one minute. Wherever you are, pause and rest in his presence.

31

YOU ARE . . .
DEFENDED

This is what the LORD says to Jerusalem:

"I will be your lawyer to plead your case,

and I will avenge you."

JEREMIAH 51:36

(If you have more time: Jeremiah 51:36-44.)

Dearest Daughter, don't worry about what other people say or think about you or your family. The Lord God promises that he will defend his children. He will be your lawyer and take up your case. He will stand up for you. We cannot always control what is said or done to us. But we can rest assured that God is working nonstop to be our defender and to prosecute those who stand against us. And at the right time, he will bring correct judgment. We do not need to take on that responsibility. God can be trusted to see it through. He does not fail.

DECLARE OUT LOUD OVER YOURSELF

The Lord is my lawyer, and he is defending me.

DECLARE OUT LOUD OVER YOUR CHILD

The Lord is [child's name]'s lawyer, and he is defending them.

CONNECT WITH YOUR HEAVENLY FATHER

What is one (or more) thing(s) you're thankful for? What is something you appreciate about who God is? Set a timer for one minute. Wherever you are, pause and rest in his presence.

32

YOU ARE . . .
KNOWN

You saw me before I was born. Every day of my

life was recorded in your book. Every moment

was laid out before a single day had passed. How

precious are your thoughts about me, O God.

They cannot be numbered!

PSALM 139:16-17

(If you have more time: Psalm 139.1-18.)

Daughter, there has never been a moment in your life when you were not loved. You have been God's delight before you even knew him here on this earth. Before you breathed your first breath, his loving gaze was already upon you. He knows every thought you will ever think, every word you will ever say, every action you will ever take. You are beautifully complex and unique because you were designed by a God whose creativity is without end. No one is like you because there is no one like your Creator.

DECLARE OUT LOUD OVER YOURSELF

All my life I have been and will be known and loved.

DECLARE OUT LOUD OVER YOUR CHILD

All [child's name]'s life, they have been and will be known and loved.

CONNECT WITH YOUR HEAVENLY FATHER

What is one (or more) thing(s) you're thankful for? What is something you appreciate about who God is? Set a timer for one minute. Wherever you are, pause and rest in his presence.

33

YOU ARE . . .
NOT OVERLOOKED

God is not unjust; he will not forget your work
and the love you have shown him as you have
helped his people and continue to help them.

HEBREWS 6:10, NIV

(If you have more time: Hebrews 6:1-12.)

Precious Mama, our daily tasks and responsibilities can seem mundane at times. We can wonder if what we are doing even makes a difference or adds up to anything much at all. But when you fold laundry, work hard to pay bills, play trucks on the floor instead of turning on the TV, choose to answer with compassion instead of anger—these things are seen by God. He receives them as love and counts them as worship. And he will not forget or overlook or discount anything—no matter the size—that is done for him or his children.

DECLARE OUT LOUD OVER YOURSELF

My hard work and my love are seen and counted by God.

DECLARE OUT LOUD OVER YOUR CHILD

[Child's name]'s hard work and their love are seen and counted by God.

CONNECT WITH YOUR HEAVENLY FATHER

What is one (or more) thing(s) you're thankful for? What is something you appreciate about who God is? Set a timer for one minute. Wherever you are, pause and rest in his presence.

I AM NOT REJECTED BY GOD. THERE IS NOTHING IN MY LIFE THAT HE CALLS RUINED.

34

YOU ARE . . .
NOT REJECTED OR RUINED

No more will anyone call you Rejected,

and your country will no more be called Ruined.

You'll be called Hephzibah (My Delight).

ISAIAH 62:4, MSG

(If you have more time: Isaiah 62:1-12.)

Mama, Joseph was rejected by his brothers. Leah was Jacob's least favorite wife. David was left out by his own father. Almost every Old Testament prophet was shunned and threatened with death. John the Baptist was considered too extreme by the "church" of the day. Many times, each of their stories seemed ruined. Even Jesus, who came down from heaven and gave up everything for his people, was rejected again and again. His own disciples thought everything was over after Jesus' death on the cross. But God has a history of seeing people and situations differently than everyone else. He delights in what the world rejects. He doesn't consider any situation ruined—just *not finished yet.*

DECLARE OUT LOUD OVER YOURSELF

I am not rejected by God. There is nothing in my life that he calls ruined.

DECLARE OUT LOUD OVER YOUR CHILD

[Child's name] is not rejected by God. There is nothing in their life that he calls ruined.

CONNECT WITH YOUR HEAVENLY FATHER

What is one (or more) thing(s) you're thankful for? What is something you appreciate about who God is? Set a timer for one minute. Wherever you are, pause and rest in his presence.

35

YOU ARE . . . WANTED

I have loved you, my people,

with an everlasting love.

With unfailing love I have

drawn you to myself.

JEREMIAH 31:3

(If you have more time: Jeremiah 31:1-14.)

Daughter, you are wanted. God doesn't just love you because he has to. He doesn't welcome you just because you showed up. He has gone to great lengths to draw you to himself. In every high and low moment of your life, he has been there. Even when you did not perceive him, God was (and still is) there, transforming your past and your future into something good. There is nothing you can do to cause him to abandon you or stop loving you. His love for you will last throughout all eternity.

DECLARE OUT LOUD OVER YOURSELF

I am wanted and loved for all eternity.

DECLARE OUT LOUD OVER YOUR CHILD

[Child's name] is wanted and loved for all eternity.

CONNECT WITH YOUR HEAVENLY FATHER

What is one (or more) thing(s) you're thankful for? What is something you appreciate about who God is? Set a timer for one minute. Wherever you are, pause and rest in his presence.

36

YOU ARE . . .
INVITED IN

My heart has heard you say,

"Come and talk with me."

And my heart responds,

"LORD, I am coming."

PSALM 27:8

(If you have more time: Psalm 27:1-14.)

Mama, God calls, "Come." This invitation is echoed again and again throughout Scripture. And today the Holy Spirit picks up the divine echo and whispers into our hearts, "Come here, my Daughter." The God of the universe *wants* to sit and talk with you. He desires to spend time with you and to hold you close, just as we do with our children. When you come into his presence, he is overjoyed. No performance is needed; no perfect words are required. Just you, responding to your Father's call to come.

DECLARE OUT LOUD OVER YOURSELF

God desires to talk and spend time with me.

DECLARE OUT LOUD OVER YOUR CHILD

God desires to talk and spend time with [child's name].

CONNECT WITH YOUR HEAVENLY FATHER

What is one (or more) thing(s) you're thankful for? What is something you appreciate about who God is? Set a timer for one minute. Wherever you are, pause and rest in his presence.

37

YOU ARE . . .
LOVED BEYOND UNDERSTANDING

I [Jesus] am in them and you [God] are in me.

May they experience such perfect unity that the

world will know that you sent me and that you

love them as much as you love me.

JOHN 17:23

(If you have more time: John 17:20-26.)

Sister-friend, God loves you as much as he loves his Son, Jesus. Can you believe that? His love is not based on our rank or our accomplishments. He doesn't love us more if we have a bigger purpose or a larger impact. God did not choose the individual plans for our lives by picking who he loved the most. Our relationship and closeness with God are determined by us, not by his level of affection. He wants you to "know this love that surpasses knowledge—that you may be filled to the measure of all the fullness of God" (Ephesians 3:19, NIV). Your heavenly Father's love for you is unfathomable.

DECLARE OUT LOUD OVER YOURSELF

God loves me as much as he loves his Son, Jesus.

DECLARE OUT LOUD OVER YOUR CHILD

God loves [child's name] as much as he loves his Son, Jesus.

CONNECT WITH YOUR HEAVENLY FATHER

What is one (or more) thing(s) you're thankful for? What is something you appreciate about who God is? Set a timer for one minute. Wherever you are, pause and rest in his presence.

38

YOU ARE . . .
FAITHFULLY LOVED

The faithful love of the LORD never ends!

His mercies never cease.

LAMENTATIONS 3:22

(If you have more time: Lamentations 3:22-32.)

Mama, there may not be a lot of faithful people or steadfast things in your life. But God's love can be trusted. It won't let you down. It is not dependent on anything or anyone else—not even you. You can build on and hide in his faithful love even when nothing else feels safe. There is nothing that can scare him off or make him change his mind about you. You can never need too much or be too much for him. His love will never run out or give up.

DECLARE OUT LOUD OVER YOURSELF

The Lord's love for me is faithful.

DECLARE OUT LOUD OVER YOUR CHILD

The Lord's love for [child's name] is faithful.

CONNECT WITH YOUR HEAVENLY FATHER

What is one (or more) thing(s) you're thankful for? What is something you appreciate about who God is? Set a timer for one minute. Wherever you are, pause and rest in his presence.

God's love can be trusted.
It won't let you down.

39

YOU ARE . . .
SECURE IN HIS LOVE

"Even if the mountains walk away and the hills fall

to pieces, my love won't walk away from you, my

covenant commitment of peace won't fall apart."

The GOD who has compassion on you says so.

ISAIAH 54:10, MSG

(If you have more time: Isaiah 54:1-10.)

There are days when we feel the abundance of God. And there are days when even the sturdiest things in our lives don't seem solid, when the safe and the familiar seem to be falling apart. But every day, God's love can be depended on. Every day his peace can hold you strong. His love won't shake; it won't loosen; it won't pull back or let go. He can be trusted in and rested on. You are safe in his love, held in his peace, and surrounded by his compassion.

DECLARE OUT LOUD OVER YOURSELF

No matter how I feel or what my circumstances are, God's love has not and will not ever walk away from me.

DECLARE OUT LOUD OVER YOUR CHILD

No matter how they feel or what their circumstances are, God's love has not and will not ever walk away from [child's name].

CONNECT WITH YOUR HEAVENLY FATHER

What is one (or more) thing(s) you're thankful for? What is something you appreciate about who God is? Set a timer for one minute. Wherever you are, pause and rest in his presence.

40

YOU ARE . . .
GUARDED

You go before me and follow me.

You place your hand of blessing on my head.

PSALM 139:5

(If you have more time: Psalm 139:1-24.)

Beloved Daughter, God leads your steps and guards your back. There is nowhere you go that he hasn't already scouted out for you, nothing you walk into that he has not already seen. He protects you on the journey and prohibits what will bring you harm. As you walk, dance, and sometimes trudge down your life's path, he places his hand upon you. God himself reaches down to bless you.

DECLARE OUT LOUD OVER YOURSELF

You go before me and follow behind me. You place your hand of blessing upon me.

DECLARE OUT LOUD OVER YOUR CHILD

You go before [child's name] and follow behind them. You place your hand of blessing upon [name].

CONNECT WITH YOUR HEAVENLY FATHER

What is one (or more) thing(s) you're thankful for? What is something you appreciate about who God is? Set a timer for one minute. Wherever you are, pause and rest in his presence.

41

YOU ARE . . .
HANDPICKED

You did not choose me, but I chose you and

appointed you so that you might go and bear

fruit—fruit that will last—and so that whatever

you ask in my name the Father will give you.

JOHN 15:16, NIV

(If you have more time: John 15:1-17.)

Daughter, God gazed across eternity and picked you. Then he chose you for a position in his Kingdom. He created you in love and designed you perfectly. Throughout your whole life, he has been calling you to him. You are not an accident. You were not appointed because you stumbled into the right spot. No one can fill the place in God's heart or plan that you have. He designed you to bear fruit that only you can produce. And he will equip you with what you need to succeed.

DECLARE OUT LOUD OVER YOURSELF

I was specifically picked and equipped by God.

DECLARE OUT LOUD OVER YOUR CHILD

[Child's name] was specifically picked and equipped by God.

CONNECT WITH YOUR HEAVENLY FATHER

What is one (or more) thing(s) you're thankful for? What is something you appreciate about who God is? Set a timer for one minute. Wherever you are, pause and rest in his presence.

42

YOU ARE . . .
CHOSEN

Because we are united with Christ, we have

received an inheritance from God, for he chose

us in advance, and he makes everything work

out according to his plan.

EPHESIANS 1:11

(If you have more time: Ephesians 1:3-11.)

Daughter of the Most High, you were divinely chosen. God prophesied about your life and wrote it all in his Book before you were even born. And not only that, but your child was specifically chosen to be your child; your relationship with and leadership of them are not random. You matter more than you could imagine. What you do—the big and small—impacts eternity. You are needed and necessary in his Kingdom and part of his eternal plan. You are important to your heavenly Father.

DECLARE OUT LOUD OVER YOURSELF

It gave God great pleasure to choose me as his own.

DECLARE OUT LOUD OVER YOUR CHILD

It gave God great pleasure to choose [child's name] as his own.

CONNECT WITH YOUR HEAVENLY FATHER

What is one (or more) thing(s) you're thankful for? What is something you appreciate about who God is? Set a timer for one minute. Wherever you are, pause and rest in his presence.

43

YOU ARE . . .
GIFTED

God in his kindness

gave each of us different gifts.

ROMANS 12:6, GW

(If you have more time: Romans 12:1-16.)

When your Father was weaving you together in your mother's womb, he wove into you your gifts, your talents, and everything that makes you, you. He doesn't want you to be like your sister, your friend, your mom, or that girl on Instagram. You will never be better than them at being them. But, Sister-friend, no one—*no one*—is better at being you than you. He designed you to fit into a place and purpose that only you can fit into. He has given you something special. Don't overlook or diminish what he trusted you with.

DECLARE OUT LOUD OVER YOURSELF

I am gifted.

DECLARE OUT LOUD OVER YOUR CHILD

[Child's name] is gifted.

CONNECT WITH YOUR HEAVENLY FATHER

What is one (or more) thing(s) you're thankful for? What is something you appreciate about who God is? Set a timer for one minute. Wherever you are, pause and rest in his presence.

44

YOU ARE . . .
AN IMPORTANT PART

What we have is one body with many parts, each its proper size and in its proper place. No part is important on its own. Can you imagine Eye telling Hand, "Get lost; I don't need you"? Or, Head telling Foot, "You're fired; your job has been phased out"? As a matter of fact, in practice it works the other way—the "lower" the part, the more basic, and therefore necessary. You can live without an eye, for instance, but not without a stomach. When it's a part of your own body you are concerned with, it makes *no* difference whether the part is visible or clothed, higher or lower. You give it dignity and honor just as it is, without comparisons. If anything, you have more concern for the lower parts than the higher. If you had to choose, wouldn't you prefer good digestion to full-bodied hair?

1 CORINTHIANS 12:20-24, MSG
(If you have more time: 1 Corinthians 12:12-27.)

Daughter, you are an important part of a unified whole. You have a purpose and a function in God's Kingdom. If you do not fulfill what he has designed you for, the whole body suffers. Your part is not insignificant; you are not disposable. The body and the Kingdom are designed to operate with you in it. Our goal isn't to become the more desirable or visible part—the stomach or the eye or the glossy head of hair—but rather to become and fulfill the part God has planned for our lives.

DECLARE OUT LOUD OVER YOURSELF

My purpose is important to God's Kingdom, and I will fulfill it.

DECLARE OUT LOUD OVER YOUR CHILD

[Child's name]'s purpose is important to God's Kingdom, and they will fulfill it.

CONNECT WITH YOUR HEAVENLY FATHER

What is one (or more) thing(s) you're thankful for? What is something you appreciate about who God is? Set a timer for one minute. Wherever you are, pause and rest in his presence.

45

YOU ARE . . .
A CHILD AND AN HEIR
OF THE MOST HIGH GOD

Since we are his children, we are his heirs.

In fact, together with Christ we are heirs of

God's glory. But if we are to share his glory,

we must also share his suffering.

ROMANS 8:17

(If you have more time: Romans 8:1-17.)

"Daughter of God." This is your most important identifier. It cannot be taken away or removed. If this is all you would ever be, it is enough. But there is more. You are also God's heir. Everything he has will become yours. Walking through the grocery store, you are an heir of eternity. Cleaning puke out of the bedsheets, you carry his glory. Teaching your children about their Father God, you are passing on your royal family heritage. Head high, Mama. Motherhood is hard, but it does not change your true identity or your eternal inheritance; in fact, it may just be refining it.

DECLARE OUT LOUD OVER YOURSELF

I am a child and an heir of the Most High God.

DECLARE OUT LOUD OVER YOUR CHILD

[Child's name] is a child and an heir of the Most High God.

CONNECT WITH YOUR HEAVENLY FATHER

What is one (or more) thing(s) you're thankful for? What is something you appreciate about who God is? Set a timer for one minute. Wherever you are, pause and rest in his presence.

46

YOU ARE . . .
PRECIOUS

Others were given in exchange for you. I traded

their lives for yours because you are precious

to me. You are honored, and I love you.

ISAIAH 43:4

(If you have more time: Isaiah 43:1-10.)

You are precious to me.
You are honored.
I love you.

The Creator of the universe left you a love note so you can remember just how much you mean to him. The Almighty God holds you in high esteem. You are treasured by him. He considers you valuable—so valuable, in fact, that his Son laid down his life to redeem you and make you his. You are worth everything he sacrificed for you; he does not regret it. Sister-friend, do you realize just how cherished and loved you are?

DECLARE OUT LOUD OVER YOURSELF

I am precious. I am honored. I am loved by the King.

DECLARE OUT LOUD OVER YOUR CHILD

[Child's name] is precious. They are honored. They are loved by the King.

CONNECT WITH YOUR HEAVENLY FATHER

What is one (or more) thing(s) you're thankful for? What is something you appreciate about who God is? Set a timer for one minute. Wherever you are, pause and rest in his presence.

YOU ARE NOT LEFT OUT, UNNOTICED, NEGLECTED, OR ALONE— **YOU BELONG TO GOD** AND ARE PART OF HIS DIVINE FAMILY.

47

YOU ARE . . .
ROYALTY

You are a chosen people. You are royal priests,

a holy nation, God's very own possession. . . .

He called you out of the darkness

into his wonderful light.

1 PETER 2:9

(If you have more time: 1 Peter 2:4-12.)

Beloved Daughter. This is your identity and the truth about who you are. You are not rejected—you have been chosen by the God of the universe. You are not common—you are of royal descent.

You are not a failure—God, the one true Judge, calls you holy.

You are not useless—you have been created with a plan and for a purpose.

You are not left out, unnoticed, neglected, or alone—you belong to God and are part of his divine family.

DECLARE OUT LOUD OVER YOURSELF

I am chosen and holy, part of God's royal lineage and family.

DECLARE OUT LOUD OVER YOUR CHILD

[Child's name] is chosen and holy, part of God's royal lineage and family.

CONNECT WITH YOUR HEAVENLY FATHER

What is one (or more) thing(s) you're thankful for? What is something you appreciate about who God is? Set a timer for one minute. Wherever you are, pause and rest in his presence.

48

YOU ARE . . .
BEAUTIFUL

Your royal husband delights in your beauty;

honor him, for he is your lord.

PSALM 45:11

(If you have more time: Psalm 45:1-17.)

The Lord God Almighty is delighted by your beauty. After viewing and creating everything seen and unseen in this world and others, he calls you beautiful. He sees all of you and knows who you truly are, and he calls you beautiful. He sees everything you have ever done and everything you will ever do, and he calls you beautiful. Through every season of your life—from baby drool, to braces, to stretch marks, to wrinkles—he calls you beautiful. God does not think of you as his obligation, his responsibility, or his duty—you are his delight.

DECLARE OUT LOUD OVER YOURSELF

God calls me beautiful.

DECLARE OUT LOUD OVER YOUR CHILD

God calls [child's name] beautiful.

CONNECT WITH YOUR HEAVENLY FATHER

What is one (or more) thing(s) you're thankful for? What is something you appreciate about who God is? Set a timer for one minute. Wherever you are, pause and rest in his presence.

49

YOU ARE . . .
FLAWLESS

You are altogether beautiful, my darling;

there is no flaw in you.

SONG OF SONGS 4:7, NIV

(If you have more time: Song of Songs 4:7-15.)

When God looks at you, he sees no flaw. You are not too loud, too quiet, too large, too small, too little, or not enough. He sees all of you; nothing is hidden from him. And still, he calls *all* of you beautiful, not just the pieces you think are right. Every part of you—the parts you like and the parts you don't—has been designed by him. Pause right now. Take a deep breath in and receive God's decree over you: "All of you is beautiful; I find no flaw in you."

DECLARE OUT LOUD OVER YOURSELF

All of me is beautiful; God has designed me without flaw.

DECLARE OUT LOUD OVER YOUR CHILD

All of [child's name] is beautiful; God has designed them without flaw.

CONNECT WITH YOUR HEAVENLY FATHER

What is one (or more) thing(s) you're thankful for? What is something you appreciate about who God is? Set a timer for one minute. Wherever you are, pause and rest in his presence.

50

YOU ARE . . .
MADE IN THE IMAGE OF GOD

God created human beings in his own image.

In the image of God he created them; male

and female he created them. . . . Then God

looked over all he had made, and he saw

that it was very good!

GENESIS 1:27, 31

(If you have more time: Genesis 1:26 31.)

Mama, you are made in the image of God. You were created to show God to the world, to bear his image on the earth. You give us a glimpse of the divine we would not see without you. The world needs to experience, see, learn, and view more of God by coming into contact with you and experiencing the "very good" that you add to creation. We know him better because of you. Your worth and value are not based on what you do, but on who you are. You are God's daughter. His traits and image are godly heirlooms passed down to the world through you.

DECLARE OUT LOUD OVER YOURSELF

I am made in the image of our great God, and he has pronounced me "very good."

DECLARE OUT LOUD OVER YOUR CHILD

[Child's name] is made in the image of our great God, and he has pronounced them "very good."

CONNECT WITH YOUR HEAVENLY FATHER

What is one (or more) thing(s) you're thankful for? What is something you appreciate about who God is? Set a timer for one minute. Wherever you are, pause and rest in his presence.

3

DIVINELY

EQUIPPED

"I FEEL LIKE I'M FAILING AT EVERYTHING," I said as Lauren's shrill screams pierced my mama heart. *This is my fault,* I told myself. *Something I'm eating is getting into my breast milk, causing her belly to seize up and send pain shooting through her body.*

Matt and I had gone to three different doctors and walked out with three different treatment plans tucked in the diaper bag. But all of the doctors agreed that our baby daughter was having trouble digesting my milk. After eliminating almost everything from my diet, I was down to eating rice, chicken, and bland vegetables (goodbye to onions, garlic, and tomatoes, among others).

We gave my daughter an assortment of all the expensive formulas that were advertised as allergen-free and promised to ease sensitive stomachs. At one point, I even made my own formula out of goat's milk and other assorted ingredients. But each one only seemed to make her screaming worse. We tried massages, sleep schedules, oils, diets, and more with no success. In my mind, I was convinced it was me. *I* was causing her pain by doing or not doing something.

I worried about the overall consequences. Was this a temporary issue? Or was this just the beginning of something she would have to deal with her whole life? By not being able to figure out a diagnosis and delaying treatment, were we making it worse? How serious was this?

• • •

I was so excited when I quit working full-time and was able to be home with my kids. Visions of crafting and playgrounds and baking swirled through my daydreams. Everything would be so much easier.

Now, I wasn't totally naïve. I knew that there would be hard times. But I had thrived in stressful situations before. If I had succeeded as a surgical nurse in life-or-death situations and as an educator working with top public health officials, I would surely be able to succeed and get everything running smoothly at home. There was no way being at home could be as demanding as that. . . .

Except that it was. In fact, it was worse.

Being a mom is hard.

No matter if you work or not, it will take everything you are and more.

Whether figuring out digestion issues, managing learning difficulties, teaching your kids to share, getting everyone's laundry folded, or having the patience to let them tie their own shoes when you're running late, it can feel like everyone needs something from us, and we don't have enough to give. It can feel like we are failing at everything.

Just today as I sat in the salon chair staring at myself in the mirror, my hairstylist voiced the same thought back at me. This mama had overcome generational curses that I couldn't even imagine. She had not only changed her own life, but she was also doing the messy, daily work of changing the future for her children and all of the generations that would follow them. As she snipped away my dead ends, she looked to the floor and said, "I'm just afraid I'm going to screw them up."

Like that tacky jingle that repeatedly interrupts our favorite playlists, it doesn't take very long until some version of this motherhood motto pops into our thoughts and conversations. And over and over again, we mamas parrot the message back in shame, "I feel like I'm messing everything up. I think I'm damaging my kids for life." Oh, Sister-friend, let's not give any more power or reach to this lie. Let us rebelliously refuse to listen silently as we and our sisters are brainwashed by the enemy's branding of motherhood.

· · ·

Return with me to Matthew 11:28-30:

> Then Jesus said, "Come to me, all of you who are weary and
> carry heavy burdens, and I will give you rest. Take my yoke
> upon you. Let me teach you, because I am humble and gentle
> at heart, and you will find rest for your souls. For my yoke is
> easy to bear, and the burden I give you is light."

At first glance, this verse seems so contrary to what we need. "Are
you weary? Come here, and I'll teach you how to be humble like me,
and then gently give you my yoke and my burden."

"Uh . . . no thanks, Jesus." I don't really want to trade one burden
for another, no matter how gently it's handed to me. And I feel humble
enough, knowing just how much I am failing. I don't need any more
reminders about how "not great" I am.

But here's the thing we don't understand: Being humble is not thinking poorly of ourselves. Jesus certainly didn't. Humility is believing
God's Word, promises, and character over everything else, even over
what we feel or see. It means that in all areas—our actions, words,
thoughts, and beliefs—we submit to his truth.

Humility means that we agree with him when he says:

Overwhelming victory is yours; you are more than a con-
queror (Romans 8:37). You are above all things and beneath no one
(Deuteronomy 28:13). When you are walking with God, you will succeed in everything you put your hands to (Deuteronomy 30:9). God
has a good future planned for you and your family (Jeremiah 29:11).
Your children will be taught by the Lord, and they will have great peace

(Isaiah 54:13). God will finish what he started in you and in your children (Philippians 1:6). You will reap a harvest if you don't give up (Galatians 6:9). You are a vessel of honor, set apart and prepared to do the good things God has planned for you (2 Timothy 2:21).

You are not failing. You are equipped and able. You are victorious. You show off his glory. You are made in the image of God.

Sister-friend, we could go on and on. Jesus' first attribute that he wants to teach to those of us who are weary and carrying heavy things is humility. He goes on to remind us that he is gentle. Which means if your thoughts are not humble and not gentle toward yourself, they are not his and should not be believed.

He continues by saying that his yoke (his way) is easy and his burden is light. How can that be? Because *what he gives, he helps to carry. It doesn't depend on us and on what our efforts alone can accomplish.*

When we humble ourselves and listen to his gentle voice, we believe:

His grace is sufficient for us (2 Corinthians 12:9). He will empower us to do what we cannot do on our own (2 Peter 1:3-4). We can rest from our weary striving, because we trust that he will work and transform all of our efforts into good (Romans 8:28).

We can relax because he promises that *he* is the One who holds it all together (Colossians 1:17), that in him we *will* produce great fruit (John 15:5), and that he will grant us what we ask for (John 15:7). And he doesn't need us to be perfect or never mess up. He promises that when we fall, we will always get back up (Proverbs 24:16).

His yoke is easy and his burden is light because our "success" in motherhood or anything else doesn't depend on our wisdom or our effort. Instead, it rests on *him* giving us all that we need in order to do what *he* calls us to do—not what everyone else wants us to do—and then *him* making it all prosper. Sister-friend, that's grace—his divine enablement for us to do what we cannot do on our own.

. . .

At first I was afraid if I let go of all I was scrambling and striving to hold together, things would get missed or start to fall apart. I worried that my family and home would be worse off and my kids would turn into monsters. It felt selfish to choose to relax my grip and give it to God, as if I was choosing personal peace at the expense of my family's order and well-being.

But when thoughts like *I'm failing* or *I'd better get it together* came to mind, I refused to dwell on them. One instance at a time, I told myself, "I am not hopping on that train." And I spoke out loud, "I do not believe that anymore. The truth is . . . (plug in applicable Bible verse here)."

As I replaced those thoughts again and again, his truth freed me from those lies, and a mindset of peace and trust became my "normal." Of course, those thoughts still pop into my head occasionally. But they no longer bully me obsessively.

Now, Sister-friend, think of yourself. What would it be like to let go of the lie that you're failing and that you're in charge of holding it all together? How would it feel to stop worrying about all that could go wrong if you don't get everything right? Could you experience more joy and peace as you go throughout your day? Could you love more unconditionally?

Truthfully, there are some days when my kids' teeth get brushed only once, and I go to bed with dishes still in the sink. But that is okay. It is not a failure. I trust that my family—and their teeth—are in the Lord's hands as I follow his directions telling me what to let go of and what to hold on to. Not only do I have greater peace, but I also have greater wisdom parenting by the Spirit, instead of by the law or by fear. He gives me more energy, ability, and creativity than I would ever have on my own, and my family reaps the benefits.

As for my daughter, God was faithful, and after many months, he led us to the right specialist with the right answer. Our baby girl was diagnosed with a self-soothing developmental delay. The doctor explained how anytime she was in pain or was upset, she wasn't able to calm back down, even after the initial problem was gone. Her "digestion problems" weren't my fault or even digestion problems at all. We started infant occupational therapy, and within a few months her health and my diet were back on track. Today, through the grace and wisdom of God and those he sent us to, you would never know she had had any difficulties as a baby.

Mama, you can't do it on your own, but that doesn't mean you're failing. You have the most wise, powerful, and loving Counselor (Isaiah 9:6) working with you. You are able because *he* is able . . . "to accomplish infinitely more than we might ask or think" (Ephesians 3:20).

Heavenly Father, we come to you in the name of your Son, Jesus. I ask right now that your Holy Word and truth would overcome the lies being spoken to your daughters. Thank you that we don't have to do anything alone. We humbly ask you for your grace to do more than we could ever do on our own, especially to parent well these children you have given us. Jesus, thank you for your Holy Spirit, who is here to guide us. You are the best Father, and we are so, so blessed to be your daughters. We love you. Amen.

THERE IS NO NEED
TO DEPEND ON
THE EFFORTS YOU
DREDGE UP FROM
WITHIN YOURSELF.
THE HOLY SPIRIT
EMPOWERS YOU
WITH GOD'S VERY
OWN RESOURCES.

51

YOU ARE . . .
EMPOWERED

I pray that from his glorious,

unlimited resources he will empower you

with inner strength through his Spirit.

EPHESIANS 3:16

(If you have more time: Ephesians 3:8-21.)

Come, Daughter. Your Father has an unlimited supply of strength and vitality. There is no need to depend on the efforts you dredge up from within yourself. The Holy Spirit empowers you with God's very own resources. As his daughter, you have access to everything that he has. You don't have to mother your children solely from your own ability or wisdom. May your lack not cause you to turn to self-condemnation but instead to remember him as your true Source in all things.

DECLARE OUT LOUD OVER YOURSELF

I am empowered with inner strength through the Holy Spirit.

DECLARE OUT LOUD OVER YOUR CHILD

[Child's name] is empowered with inner strength through the Holy Spirit.

CONNECT WITH YOUR HEAVENLY FATHER

What is one (or more) thing(s) you're thankful for? What is something you appreciate about who God is? Set a timer for one minute. Wherever you are, pause and rest in his presence.

52

YOU ARE . . .
GIVEN THE RIGHT DESIRES

God is working in you, giving you the desire

and the power to do what pleases him.

PHILIPPIANS 2:13

(If you have more time: Philippians 2:12-18.)

Sister-friend, the power and ability we need do not come from us alone. Thank God that the right desires don't even need to come solely from us. Because if I'm being honest, I don't always *want* to do the right thing. Sometimes I want to be harsh with my children when they throw a fit in public. Sometimes when I'm reading, I want to ignore their requests for math help. And I don't always want to pay for private bass lessons when it means I can't afford the latest on-trend shoes. But God is transforming each one of us, and he promises that when we let him work in us, he will change even our desires to what pleases him. (RIP to my shoe collection!)

DECLARE OUT LOUD OVER YOURSELF

With God's help, I have the desire and the ability to do what he is calling me to do.

DECLARE OUT LOUD OVER YOUR CHILD

With God's help, [child's name] has the desire and the ability to do what he is calling them to do.

CONNECT WITH YOUR HEAVENLY FATHER

What is one (or more) thing(s) you're thankful for? What is something you appreciate about who God is? Set a timer for one minute. Wherever you are, pause and rest in his presence.

53

YOU ARE . . .
ABLE

With God's power working in us,

God can do much, much more than

anything we can ask or imagine.

EPHESIANS 3:20, NCV

(If you have more time: Ephesians 3:14-20.)

Daughter, in him you are stronger than you know. And through his Spirit you are becoming so much more than you could ever believe. The infinite power of God is working within you. It is his strength that will enable you to carry out what he has called you to do and to be for your family. Sister-friend, you cannot even fathom the heights he wants to take you to. May he increase your boldness to ask and believe for the largeness of what he wants to give you. With his mighty power at work within you, even your wildest dreams are infinitely too small.

DECLARE OUT LOUD OVER YOURSELF

Because God is working in me, I am able to do more than I could ever imagine.

DECLARE OUT LOUD OVER YOUR CHILD

Because God is working in [child's name], they are able to do more than they could ever imagine.

CONNECT WITH YOUR HEAVENLY FATHER

What is one (or more) thing(s) you're thankful for? What is something you appreciate about who God is? Set a timer for one minute. Wherever you are, pause and rest in his presence.

54

YOU ARE . . . GRACED

Today I am who I am because of God's grace,
and *I have made sure that* the grace He offered
me has not been wasted. I have worked harder,
longer, and smarter than all the rest; but
I realize it is not me—it is God's grace with me
that has made the difference.

1 CORINTHIANS 15:10, THE VOICE
(If you have more time: 1 Corinthians 15:1-11.)

Mama, God's grace empowers us. Through it, we have access to what is beyond us. We can go past our own natural ability, knowledge, and endurance because of his grace. This means we can ask and receive by faith the patience we need to teach and correct our children, the wisdom and solutions we need for every situation and the deep questions they have, the energy and direction to thrive and to accomplish all we need to do, and so much more. God's gift of grace to us makes all the difference.

DECLARE OUT LOUD OVER YOURSELF

I can work harder, longer, smarter, and with more productivity and results because of God's grace in me.

DECLARE OUT LOUD OVER YOUR CHILD

[Child's name] can work harder, longer, smarter, and with more productivity and results because of God's grace in them.

CONNECT WITH YOUR HEAVENLY FATHER

What is one (or more) thing(s) you're thankful for? What is something you appreciate about who God is? Set a timer for one minute. Wherever you are, pause and rest in his presence.

55

YOU ARE . . . SUPPLIED

My God will liberally supply (fill until full)

your every need according to His riches

in glory in Christ Jesus.

PHILIPPIANS 4:19, AMP

(If you have more time: Philippians 4:10-20.)

Oh, Mama, have peace that God knows your needs. He designed motherhood to be done with him. When you were formed in your mother's womb, he called you "fearfully and wonderfully made" (Psalm 139:14, NIV), not because you were complete and without need but because you were exactly how he wanted you to be. He will joyfully and generously give you everything you require according to his abundance, not ours.

DECLARE OUT LOUD OVER YOURSELF

God is giving me everything I need according to his abundant supply.

DECLARE OUT LOUD OVER YOUR CHILD

God is giving [child's name] everything they need according to his abundant supply.

CONNECT WITH YOUR HEAVENLY FATHER

What is one (or more) thing(s) you're thankful for? What is something you appreciate about who God is? Set a timer for one minute. Wherever you are, pause and rest in his presence.

56

YOU ARE . . .
PROVIDED FOR

Seek the Kingdom of God above all else,

and live righteously, and he will give you

everything you need.

MATTHEW 6:33

(If you have more time: Matthew 6:19-34.)

Chosen Mama, it can feel like there are more things to do than we have time and energy for. The demands are exhausting, and it is tempting to rush or skip things that carry eternal weight but not immediate results. Laundry, dishes, and toilet cleaning seem more productive than time spent praying, using our talents, or being with our children. It can be scary to reprioritize our to-do list and put God's things first. But he promises that when we do, he will provide everything we need (the energy, the time, and the resources).

DECLARE OUT LOUD OVER YOURSELF

I will make your Kingdom and your order my first priorities, and you will provide everything I need.

DECLARE OUT LOUD OVER YOUR CHILD

[Child's name] will make your Kingdom and your order their first priorities, and you will provide everything they need.

CONNECT WITH YOUR HEAVENLY FATHER

What is one (or more) thing(s) you're thankful for? What is something you appreciate about who God is? Set a timer for one minute. Wherever you are, pause and rest in his presence.

It is tempting to rush or
skip things that carry
eternal weight but not
immediate results.

57

YOU ARE . . .
HEARD

You heard me when I cried,

"Listen to my pleading! Hear my cry for help!"

Yes, you came when I called; you told me,

"Do not fear."

LAMENTATIONS 3:56-57

(If you have more time: Lamentations 3:49-58.)

Daughter, he hears you. He responds to your voice and your pleadings. When you tell him you need help, he comes to your side. He will not downplay your cries or say you are overreacting. He will never leave you alone, even if the pain is from the consequences of your own disobedience. No, he comes near and reassures you: "There is no need to fear. I heard you, and I came. I am here with you." You are heard. You are seen. You are not alone.

DECLARE OUT LOUD OVER YOURSELF

The Lord hears me and comes quickly to help.

DECLARE OUT LOUD OVER YOUR CHILD

The Lord hears [child's name] and comes quickly to help.

CONNECT WITH YOUR HEAVENLY FATHER

What is one (or more) thing(s) you're thankful for? What is something you appreciate about who God is? Set a timer for one minute. Wherever you are, pause and rest in his presence.

58

YOU ARE . . .
GIVEN GOOD THINGS

Keep on asking, and you will receive what you ask for. Keep on seeking, and you will find. Keep on knocking, and the door will be opened to you. For everyone who asks, receives. Everyone who seeks, finds. And to everyone who knocks, the door will be opened. . . . If you sinful people know how to give good gifts to your children, how much more will your heavenly Father give good gifts to those who ask him.

MATTHEW 7:7-8, 11

(If you have more time: Matthew 7:1-11.)

Daughter, your Father is not trying to trick you. He is not looking for ways to trap you into deals at your expense or sign you up for a loan with hidden fees. Too often we come to him with open hands and cringing hearts, waiting to see how he responds to our prayers. But he wants to give you *good things*. So don't give up if you haven't received what you need yet; keep asking. Your heavenly Father loves to give good gifts to his children.

DECLARE OUT LOUD OVER YOURSELF

I will receive good things when I ask God.

DECLARE OUT LOUD OVER YOUR CHILD

[Child's name] will receive good things when they ask God.

CONNECT WITH YOUR HEAVENLY FATHER

What is one (or more) thing(s) you're thankful for? What is something you appreciate about who God is? Set a timer for one minute. Wherever you are, pause and rest in his presence.

59

YOU ARE . . .
NOT RUINING EVERYTHING

And we know that in all things God works for

the good of those who love him, who have been

called according to his purpose.

ROMANS 8:28, NIV

(If you have more time: Romans 8:26-39.)

There is nothing God won't change into good for you and your children. "All things" includes our weaknesses, mess-ups, and missed opportunities. It means that when we get it wrong, God doesn't say, "I'll make sure this doesn't do too much damage." He says, "I'm going to turn this into something beautiful and beneficial." So exhale. Let it go. Let God have it. He will transform it into something so good.

DECLARE OUT LOUD OVER YOURSELF

God is transforming all things, even my weaknesses, into something good for me and my children.

DECLARE OUT LOUD OVER YOUR CHILD

God is transforming all things, even [child's name]'s weaknesses, into something good for them.

CONNECT WITH YOUR HEAVENLY FATHER

What is one (or more) thing(s) you're thankful for? What is something you appreciate about who God is? Set a timer for one minute. Wherever you are, pause and rest in his presence.

60

YOU ARE . . .
NOT FAILING WHEN IT'S HARD

Don't look for shortcuts to God. The market is

flooded with surefire, easygoing formulas for

a successful life that can be practiced in your

spare time. Don't fall for that stuff, even though

crowds of people do. The way to life—to God!—

is vigorous and requires total attention.

MATTHEW 7:13-14, MSG

(If you have more time: Matthew 7:13-23.)

Mama, just because it's hard doesn't mean you're doing it wrong. We scorn athletes who don't break a sweat, take a few hits, or "leave it all on the field." But we feel like we're failures when our cars are a mess, our bodies are exhausted, and our results don't match the promises online saying "do this to be as happy and breezy as me." The Word of God tells us the opposite though. Breaking generational curses and building Kingdom legacies require hard work, dedication, and sacrifice. But through his grace, we can do it. So don't get discouraged. Head up. You're doing okay, Mama.

DECLARE OUT LOUD OVER YOURSELF

I am not failing; I am working hard to build God's Kingdom here.

DECLARE OUT LOUD OVER YOUR CHILD

[Child's name] is not failing; they are working hard to build God's Kingdom here.

CONNECT WITH YOUR HEAVENLY FATHER

What is one (or more) thing(s) you're thankful for? What is something you appreciate about who God is? Set a timer for one minute. Wherever you are, pause and rest in his presence.

61

YOU ARE . . .
STRONG IN YOUR WEAKNESS

Each time he said, "My grace is all you need. My power works best in weakness." So now I am glad to boast about my weaknesses, so that the power of Christ can work through me. That's why I take pleasure in my weaknesses, and in the insults, hardships, persecutions, and troubles that I suffer for Christ. For when I am weak, then I am strong.

2 CORINTHIANS 12:9-10

(If you have more time: 2 Corinthians 12:1-10.)

Our weaknesses can haunt us, sneaking around and whispering horrible things into our broken places. But our Father works best in the areas that we are embarrassed and ashamed of. Our shortcomings are his places of strength. Our humanness is where he shines through the most. His ability and grace become obvious when we reach the end of our patience, energy, and knowledge and call upon his reserves. When we cry out in our emptiness, it's easy to see that *he* is what holds us together and empowers us. He does not despise our weaknesses. It is there that we become channels of his strength.

DECLARE OUT LOUD OVER YOURSELF

The power of Christ is working through and seen in my weaknesses.

DECLARE OUT LOUD OVER YOUR CHILD

The power of Christ is working through and seen in [child's name]'s weaknesses.

CONNECT WITH YOUR HEAVENLY FATHER

What is one (or more) thing(s) you're thankful for? What is something you appreciate about who God is? Set a timer for one minute. Wherever you are, pause and rest in his presence.

GOD CALLS YOU TO HIMSELF

WHEN YOU HAVE NOTHING LEFT TO GIVE, SO THAT *HE* CAN GIVE TO *YOU*.

62

YOU ARE . . .
FILLED

Is anyone thirsty? Come and drink—

even if you have no money!

Come, take your choice of wine or milk—

it's all free!

ISAIAH 55:1

(If you have more time: Isaiah 55:1-13.)

Mama, is your soul thirsty? God calls you to come—not so that you can receive condemnation or anything more to add to your to-do or to-fix or to-work-on lists. He says, "Come," in order that you may be filled. He calls you to himself when you have nothing left to give, so that *he* can give to *you*. You aren't required to purchase his refreshment or supply of grace with your own efforts. They are freely given to you by your Father.

DECLARE OUT LOUD OVER YOURSELF

God is refreshing and refilling me.

DECLARE OUT LOUD OVER YOUR CHILD

God is refreshing and refilling [child's name].

CONNECT WITH YOUR HEAVENLY FATHER

What is one (or more) thing(s) you're thankful for? What is something you appreciate about who God is? Set a timer for one minute. Wherever you are, pause and rest in his presence.

63

YOU ARE . . . GIVEN REST

Jesus said, "Come to me, all of you who are weary and carry heavy burdens, and I will give you rest. Take my yoke upon you. Let me teach you, because I am humble and gentle at heart, and you will find rest for your souls."

MATTHEW 11:28-29

(If you have more time: Matthew 11:25-30.)

Oh, Sister, yes, our bodies are tired. But more exhausting than the physical demands of motherhood are its emotional and mental ones. Our very souls can become weary and burdened by loads we were given but were never meant to carry alone. Jesus' way—asking, then trusting, and letting him do what only he can do—brings our souls rest. In him, churning minds and striving hearts find quietness and peace.

DECLARE OUT LOUD OVER YOURSELF

You give rest to my soul.

DECLARE OUT LOUD OVER YOUR CHILD

You give rest to [child's name]'s soul.

CONNECT WITH YOUR HEAVENLY FATHER

What is one (or more) thing(s) you're thankful for? What is something you appreciate about who God is? Set a timer for one minute. Wherever you are, pause and rest in his presence.

64

YOU ARE . . .
GIVEN WISDOM

If you need wisdom, ask our generous God,

and he will give it to you. He will not

rebuke you for asking.

JAMES 1:5

(If you have more time: James 1:1-12.)

Mama, there will be times when you don't have the right answer. You will not always know what to do or maybe even what the real root problem of a situation is. But God knows all of it and is more loving and patient than we could ever hope to be. He is generous when we ask for his wisdom. And he gives it without making us feel guilty or ashamed for not knowing the answer on our own. We can trust and rest in the fact that our parenting and our success in any area does not depend on our limited knowledge and understanding.

DECLARE OUT LOUD OVER YOURSELF

Almighty God gives me the wisdom I need for every situation and person.

DECLARE OUT LOUD OVER YOUR CHILD

Almighty God gives [child's name] the wisdom they need for every situation and person.

CONNECT WITH YOUR HEAVENLY FATHER

What is one (or more) thing(s) you're thankful for? What is something you appreciate about who God is? Set a timer for one minute. Wherever you are, pause and rest in his presence.

65

YOU ARE . . . DIRECTED

Your own ears will hear him. Right behind you
a voice will say, "This is the way you should go,"
whether to the right or to the left.

ISAIAH 30:21

(If you have more time: Isaiah 30:18-33.)

Daughter, God will give you the directions that you need. It does not all depend on you to figure out what is right or best. He promises to lead you and guide you. And not just theoretically but with clear directions in specific circumstances. The ears of your heart know the voice of their Creator. His voice will bring peace to your spirit, and his words always match the Word. Your Father desires to help you and teach you what you need to know. He will not lead you into confusion or chaos.

DECLARE OUT LOUD OVER YOURSELF

I will receive God's direction for what I should do.

DECLARE OUT LOUD OVER YOUR CHILD

[Child's name] will receive God's direction for what they should do.

CONNECT WITH YOUR HEAVENLY FATHER

What is one (or more) thing(s) you're thankful for? What is something you appreciate about who God is? Set a timer for one minute. Wherever you are, pause and rest in his presence.

66

YOU ARE . . .
GUIDED

The LORD directs the steps of the godly.

He delights in every detail of their lives.

PSALM 37:23

(If you have more time: Psalm 37:23-40.)

The Lord will direct and order your life and your days. He knows the best path to take and the best uses of your time. And he will help you in any area you invite him into—homeschooling your children, creating spreadsheets, starting IVs, sorting laundry, establishing a time management plan, and more. He delights in every detail of your life, even—and sometimes especially—the smallest ones. Precious Daughter, he wants to join you wherever you are and bring his blessings and wisdom.

DECLARE OUT LOUD OVER YOURSELF

The Lord guides and joins me in every part of my life.

DECLARE OUT LOUD OVER YOUR CHILD

The Lord guides and joins [child's name] in every part of their life.

CONNECT WITH YOUR HEAVENLY FATHER

What is one (or more) thing(s) you're thankful for? What is something you appreciate about who God is? Set a timer for one minute. Wherever you are, pause and rest in his presence.

He will help you in any area
you invite him into.

67

YOU ARE . . .
BEING LED

Seek his will in all you do,

and he will show you which path to take.

PROVERBS 3:6

(If you have more time: Proverbs 3:1-8.)

Mama, God has not left you to figure out everything by yourself. Your family's direction does not have to rest solely on your shoulders or be deduced by your brain alone. We are promised divine help. God alone can see all the roadblocks and dangers—and also the paths leading to the best-case scenarios. Our understanding is limited, but the One who knows everything promises to help us plot the course. His peace will be our guide.

DECLARE OUT LOUD OVER YOURSELF

God shows me the best path to take.

DECLARE OUT LOUD OVER YOUR CHILD

God shows [child's name] the best path to take.

CONNECT WITH YOUR HEAVENLY FATHER

What is one (or more) thing(s) you're thankful for? What is something you appreciate about who God is? Set a timer for one minute. Wherever you are, pause and rest in his presence.

68

YOU ARE . . .
POSSESSING THE LAND

Be strong and courageous, for you are the one

who will lead these people to possess all the land

I swore to their ancestors I would give them.

JOSHUA 1:6

(If you have more time: Joshua 1:1-9.)

Mama, be strong and courageous! You are called to lead your children to possess all the promises and blessings they are to inherit. You were intentionally chosen for your children to be the guide who helps them receive everything God purchased for them. But you don't have to do it alone or in your own strength. You were assigned and therefore equipped by Almighty God to accomplish this and help take the land.

DECLARE OUT LOUD OVER YOURSELF

With God's help, I will lead my children and this generation to attain all God has for them.

DECLARE OUT LOUD OVER YOUR CHILD

With God's help, [child's name] will lead their generation and attain all God has for them.

CONNECT WITH YOUR HEAVENLY FATHER

What is one (or more) thing(s) you're thankful for? What is something you appreciate about who God is? Set a timer for one minute. Wherever you are, pause and rest in his presence.

69

YOU ARE . . . SUCCESSFUL

The LORD your God will then make you
successful in everything you do. He will give you
many children and numerous livestock, and
he will cause your fields to produce abundant
harvests, for the LORD will again delight in being
good to you as he was to your ancestors.

DEUTERONOMY 30:9

(If you have more time: Deuteronomy 30:1-10.)

God's ways work. When we follow him, there are no maybes or hopefullys or want-tos. God *will* fulfill his promises to you. No circumstances or bank accounts or generational curses are more powerful than God's Word. He will cause you to be successful in *everything* you do. You will produce abundant harvests in your parenting, workplace, business start-ups, schooling, self-improvement, and anything else he calls you to sow and invest in. With God, we reap what we sow and then some. Sister-friend, you have the ability and backing to do what you have been called to do.

DECLARE OUT LOUD OVER YOURSELF

I will be successful and produce a harvest in everything God calls me to.

DECLARE OUT LOUD OVER YOUR CHILD

[Child's name] will be successful and produce a harvest in everything God calls them to.

CONNECT WITH YOUR HEAVENLY FATHER

What is one (or more) thing(s) you're thankful for? What is something you appreciate about who God is? Set a timer for one minute. Wherever you are, pause and rest in his presence.

70

YOU ARE . . .
A HARVESTER

Let us not grow weary *or*

become discouraged in doing good,

for at the proper time we will reap,

if we do not give in.

GALATIANS 6:9, AMP

(If you have more time: Galatians 6:1-10.)

Oh, Sister-friend, I know it is easy to get discouraged when everything is still a mess—when despite your best efforts and doing what God's Word says, your littles are still fighting, you're still losing your temper, your bank account is still barely enough, and your heart is still aching for what you haven't yet received. Your Father knows that the middle times are hard. But he also promises that your harvest is coming—and that it will be at just the right time. So don't give up, Mama. He won't forget or waste anything you have planted.

DECLARE OUT LOUD OVER YOURSELF

I will receive the blessing of the good things I am planting.

DECLARE OUT LOUD OVER YOUR CHILD

[Child's name] will receive the blessing of the good things they are planting.

CONNECT WITH YOUR HEAVENLY FATHER

What is one (or more) thing(s) you're thankful for? What is something you appreciate about who God is? Set a timer for one minute. Wherever you are, pause and rest in his presence.

71

YOU ARE . . .
PRODUCTIVE

And the seeds that fell on the good soil

represent honest, good-hearted people who

hear God's word, cling to it, and patiently

produce a huge harvest.

LUKE 8:15

(If you have more time: Luke 8:4-15.)

Mama, what you are doing will yield results. Motherhood can test our belief in God's promises, but we cannot focus only on what our eyes currently see. We must stubbornly and defiantly cling to his Word. As we patiently and steadfastly yield to the growth that he brings, God will trade our blurred sight for his eternal vision. He is working even now to produce a large harvest in your life, in your children's lives, and in this world.

DECLARE OUT LOUD OVER YOURSELF

My heart is good soil, and I will produce a huge harvest.

DECLARE OUT LOUD OVER YOUR CHILD

[Child's name]'s heart is good soil, and they will produce a huge harvest.

CONNECT WITH YOUR HEAVENLY FATHER

What is one (or more) thing(s) you're thankful for? What is something you appreciate about who God is? Set a timer for one minute. Wherever you are, pause and rest in his presence.

RESULTS ARE GOD'S JOB, NOT OURS.

72

YOU ARE . . .
ONLY RESPONSIBLE
FOR YOUR PART

I planted the seed in your hearts, and Apollos

watered it, but it was God who made it grow.

1 CORINTHIANS 3:6

(If you have more time: 1 Corinthians 3:1-9.)

Precious Daughter, it is God who causes your seeds—efforts—to grow. We are called to do our best—to plant and to water. But that is all that is required of us. Results are God's job, not ours. When we are faithful to do our part and not someone else's, we can rest in the fact that God controls everything else. We do not need to manipulate the process or soil, or worry if our work was enough. We can place it in God's hands. Our hearts can be at peace in knowing we are not the One who is responsible for the growth of fruit.

DECLARE OUT LOUD OVER YOURSELF

I am only responsible for my obedience; God will take care of the outcome.

DECLARE OUT LOUD OVER YOUR CHILD

[Child's name] is only responsible for their obedience; God will take care of the outcome.

CONNECT WITH YOUR HEAVENLY FATHER

What is one (or more) thing(s) you're thankful for? What is something you appreciate about who God is? Set a timer for one minute. Wherever you are, pause and rest in his presence.

73

YOU ARE . . .
VICTORIOUS

"No weapon that is formed against you will
succeed; and you will condemn every tongue
that accuses you in judgment. This is the
heritage of the servants of the LORD, and their
vindication is from Me," declares the LORD.

ISAIAH 54:17, NASB

(If you have more time: Isaiah 54:11-17.)

Slow down and reread that whole verse. Take in *all* of the promises contained in it. Nothing meant to harm or destroy you will succeed in doing so. Every accusing voice will be proved wrong. *Every voice*: The enemy's whispers in your ear, the people who pass judgment on you and your family, and even your own harsh and punishing accusations of yourself will be proved wrong. Your defense has been assigned to the Commander of Angel Armies. God Almighty is in charge of clearing your name and securing your victory. This is your heavenly birthright as a child of God.

DECLARE OUT LOUD OVER YOURSELF

Nothing will succeed against me. Every voice that accuses me will be silenced. The Lord himself justifies me and brings me victory.

DECLARE OUT LOUD OVER YOUR CHILD

Nothing will succeed against [child's name]. Every voice that accuses [name] will be silenced. The Lord himself justifies them and brings them victory.

CONNECT WITH YOUR HEAVENLY FATHER

What is one (or more) thing(s) you're thankful for? What is something you appreciate about who God is? Set a timer for one minute. Wherever you are, pause and rest in his presence.

74

YOU ARE . . .
NOT IN CHARGE OF
HOLDING IT ALL TOGETHER

He is before all things,

and in him all things hold together.

COLOSSIANS 1:17, NIV

(If you have more time: Colossians 1:15-20.)

Mama, it is easy to believe that *we* are the ones who keep everything from falling apart, that our frenzied efforts are the glue that keeps the pieces in place. We can be afraid that letting even one thing slip will trigger an avalanche effect, bringing it all down and burying us beneath the weight of failure. But God's Word promises that *Jesus* is the One who holds it all together, not us. We do not have that ability; we were never meant to carry that burden. Sister, trust that he is wiser, more powerful, and more loving than we could ever hope to be.

DECLARE OUT LOUD OVER YOURSELF

God will hold everything together for me.

DECLARE OUT LOUD OVER YOUR CHILD

God will hold everything together for [child's name].

CONNECT WITH YOUR HEAVENLY FATHER

What is one (or more) thing(s) you're thankful for? What is something you appreciate about who God is? Set a timer for one minute. Wherever you are, pause and rest in his presence.

75

YOU ARE . . .
NOT FINISHED YET

I am certain that God, who began the good work

within you, will continue his work until it is finally

finished on the day when Christ Jesus returns.

PHILIPPIANS 1:6

(If you have more time: Philippians 1:3-11.)

Sister-friend, God has not decided that "this" (whatever your "this" currently is) is good enough and moved on to another person or another focus. He does not get distracted or enticed away from his children or his plans for them. Your heavenly Father won't become discouraged and give up when the process is slow or the results aren't visible. You can trust that his glorious plan for you, your children, and your family will never be done until every detail is finished, every darkness banished, every chain broken, every hope fulfilled, and every prayer finally answered. He is not done yet.

DECLARE OUT LOUD OVER YOURSELF

God began a glorious work in me, and he will finish it.

DECLARE OUT LOUD OVER YOUR CHILD

God began a glorious work in [child's name], and he will finish it.

CONNECT WITH YOUR HEAVENLY FATHER

What is one (or more) thing(s) you're thankful for? What is something you appreciate about who God is? Set a timer for one minute. Wherever you are, pause and rest in his presence.

4

KINGDOM

CALLED

I NEED AIR. I FELT LIKE ALICE IN WONDERLAND after devouring the wrong bit of sweetness and finding herself being squeezed and squished by too little of a house. Or like I had found myself in the trash compactor with Luke, Leia, Chewie, and Han, struggling as the walls were slowly closing in on us.

I couldn't figure out if I was growing larger or everything else was growing smaller. Were the walls getting closer, or was I just getting restless? If only there were something I could swallow or a droid I could call to fix all this.

Our family of five was in a two-bedroom, eleven-hundred-square-foot, double-wide trailer. It was a step up from my in-laws' basement that we had moved out of nearly a year earlier. But still, all of my stuff—literal and figurative—was spilling out from under couches, shoved tightly into closets, or stacked up in unlikely places (thank you, Pinterest and IKEA, for all your "small spaces" ideas).

My home, my budget, my task list, my relationships, and my hope were all too small, too tight. Is it possible to be claustrophobic in your own life?

• • •

I grew up in the Midwest in a large house, with a large yard, surrounded by even larger fields. We were five country-raised children. My mom laughs when she tells stories of how farmers would drive by and joke about the half-naked Copple kids "runnin' through the grass and peein' on the trees." We three girls were the oldest, with two younger brothers rounding out the pack—just to be clear, they were the ones "peein' on the trees."

There was always somewhere to roam or explore, always a new adventure to find. The little creek down our gravel road had crawdads.

The old corncrib had booby traps. There was buried treasure—Indian Head pennies—in the yard. Our forest (two parallel rows of pine trees at the back of our property) was a kingdom teaming with villains, and we argued endlessly about which sister got to be the princess and which two became her maidservants. But we all agreed that Queen Anne's lace and purple chicory flowers braided together made the best crowns.

What we adventurers couldn't find on-site, we found in books. At night before bed, Dad read to us, and we joined famous gunfighters of the West, superheroes discovering who they really were, girls who hid from Nazis, and boys who took down giants.

We climbed just about everything: trees, the chicken house roof, the grain silos, abandoned cars, and that rotting corncrib. But the best view was from the flat roof of our house. (Don't worry, we used the pull-down stairs in the attic to reach the top.) On the Fourth of July, you could see the fireworks from three different towns up there.

The world was large, and I loved the safety of feelin' small. There was something comforting about it. I knew "the peace of wild things,"[1] as Wendell Berry wrote it, or the faith of the "birds of the air and lilies of the field,"[2] as Dad read it.

There was a great big world out there. And I was excited about what an adventure it all would be!

But then I grew big and everything got smaller.

• • •

I went to nursing school, took a job in surgery, and married my high school sweetheart, Matt. We praised God when we had our son, Gabe,

---

[1] Wendell Berry, *The Peace of Wild Things* (New York: Penguin, 2018), 25.
[2] See Matthew 6:26, 28, ESV

and daughter, Natalie. They were light and joy, my very favorite things in life. But despite my love and delight in them, the life I had built—and was told I should have—seemed so much smaller than what I had dreamed about as a child, and not nearly as exciting as all the adventures I had planned.

And then everything got even smaller. We had been bouncing from small house to small house, homes with no yards or places to explore, when due to personal bad choices and a bad economy, we declared bankruptcy, foreclosed on our town house, and moved into my in-laws' basement. That time and place was darker and harder than I can explain, and yet it saved us in so many ways. We got back on track—financially and spiritually—and we began to rebuild our lives. *Now*, I thought, *our real adventure is going to start.*

We were able to pay cash for a double-wide trailer. And not long after that, our family of four turned into five. Even though we were on track, our finances were still tight. We were on food stamps and in the WIC program, and I extreme couponed to make ends meet while Matt went to nursing school. My son could repeat back to me our lunchtime mantra: "We eat what goes bad first."

When Matt graduated and started a nursing job, I changed my hours and became a stay-at-home mom. I hoped *this* was the adventure I had wanted for so long. But as much as I loved our family and was so grateful for our trailer, the eleven-hundred-square-foot space got tighter and tighter. We frequently visited parks, malls, and friends' houses trying to find fresh air and new experiences. I was trying so hard to talk myself into being fulfilled by this life I was living, but more and more it wasn't working.

One day when I was feeling particularly compressed, I left Matt with

the kids, got in the car, and began driving the open country. Surrounded by farms as far as the eye could see, I pulled over to the side of the gravel road and got out. I picked Queen Anne's lace and purple chicory flowers from the ditch and braided them into a crown. Tears began to roll down my face as I looked out over an unplanted field.

This was not a great adventure. My world was not as large as I always believed it was.

There was no room left to dream. And I had no hope left that buried treasure could be found in the next field or season.

I thought my life would be something more than this. I was disappointed.

I felt too big for my own life.

• • •

Recently I was thinking about the parable of the three servants in Matthew 25:14-30. When their master left on a trip, all three were entrusted with "talents"—bags of silver—with the first two servants receiving the most. These two invested their money and multiplied it. But the third servant simply buried his bag in the ground.

I wondered, *Did he believe he was doing a good thing, a safe thing?*

Maybe he didn't think that his master actually expected anything out of him, especially since he had received the smallest amount of all. *What difference could that small amount even make?*

Is it possible that he didn't want to hope—that it was easier to believe a higher calling or a bigger purpose was all just a fantasy? Could it be that he was waiting for a clearer sign or more explicit directions from someone to get started?

Maybe he also looked out over empty fields, staring at where his bag of silver was buried and lamenting, "I thought my assignment—my life—would be something more than this. This is a disappointment."

Perhaps he had deceived himself so much that he was shocked hearing the other servants report to the master about their increases, thinking, *I didn't know we could do that. No one gave me instructions on how to invest it. They must have known more, had more, been more than me. How did they dare to try for something greater?*

I can picture his embarrassment and shame when it was his turn. Quickly grabbing excuses to explain his behavior, he essentially said, "I saw you as a harsh master, and I was afraid of messing up."

· · ·

Like that servant, I didn't really understand God or what he wanted from me. He appeared to be unfairly blessing others. And after everything I had been through, he seemed harsh, and I was afraid of messing up again. So I tried to be happy and settled with just what I was given.

But it wasn't working. I wanted to make a life for my children that was vast and full, even if our space was small. I wanted to believe again that anything was possible, life was limitless, and God could do more than anything I dared to ask or dream or even imagine. I longed to do something large and also to find once again that I was small and could rest in "the peace of wild things."

So staring at the barren field that day, I told God I wasn't satisfied with my life and I wanted something more. And he told me he did too. It may seem selfish to want that, but the truth is I am made for more than what this world has told me to settle for.

And so are you.

You are an indispensable part of something bigger. You were created for multiplication and abundance. He longs to give you the "much more" (Matthew 25:23, TLB) that the master promised the servants who *used* what they had been given.

So what does all that mean in real life? Should you write a book (like he called me to do), start a business, quit your job to become a full-time mom, or simply stay right where you are? I don't know. But God does. He knows what you are made for and what purpose you are meant to fulfill.

In the beginning, we were charged with being God's delegates and governors on earth, ensuring his order and rule, bringing his peace, joy, and rightness to all things. The enemy will claim that Adam's fall changed God's plan, that you don't need to do anything but bury what God gave you. But Jesus restored our original purpose, and you were given a "talent" for a reason (Ephesians 2:10).

Step into it.

Let's not stare any longer at an empty field of buried talents, feeling disappointed and too big for our lives. You have been chosen for more. Sister-friend, you are meant to play a part in his Kingdom coming and his will being done right here on earth, as it is in heaven (Matthew 6:10).

Father God, in the name of your firstborn Son, Jesus, we come to you. Forgive us for the times and places where we have settled and buried what you wanted us to multiply. We feel deep in our spirits that you have made us for more. Today we respond to the call and the longing you have placed within us. Thank you for choosing us and creating us with and for a purpose. We trust you with our dreams and our desires. Amen.

GOD MADE ME THE WAY I AM FOR A REASON, AND I HAVE AN INDISPENSABLE ROLE IN HIS KINGDOM.

76

YOU ARE . . .
HOW YOU ARE ON PURPOSE

God has made us what we are. He has created us

in Christ Jesus to live lives filled with good works

that he has prepared for us to do.

EPHESIANS 2:10, GW

(If you have more time: Ephesians 2:1-10.)

Oh, Daughter, don't you know that God created you the way you are on purpose? Your body, your soul (thoughts, will, and emotions), and your spirit are the exact way they are supposed to be in order to fulfill the plan he has. You were not meant to be strong where others are strong, or weak where others are weak. Every detail of you is known and created perfectly. Even the areas that your Father seeks to transform will prepare you for the indispensable role you have in his Kingdom. You are uniquely needed and appreciated.

DECLARE OUT LOUD OVER YOURSELF

God made me the way I am for a reason, and I have an indispensable role in his Kingdom.

DECLARE OUT LOUD OVER YOUR CHILD

God made [child's name] the way they are for a reason, and they have an indispensable role in his Kingdom.

CONNECT WITH YOUR HEAVENLY FATHER

What is one (or more) thing(s) you're thankful for? What is something you appreciate about who God is? Set a timer for one minute. Wherever you are, pause and rest in his presence.

77

YOU ARE . . .
ENCOURAGED TO
USE YOUR GIFT

The master was furious. "That's a terrible way to live! It's criminal to live cautiously like that! If you knew I was after the best, why did you do less than the least? The least you could have done would have been to invest the sum with the bankers, where at least I would have gotten a little interest."

MATTHEW 25:26-27, MSG

(If you have more time: Matthew 25:14-30.)

Precious Daughter, life can be busy and motherhood can be demanding, but the Lord has given you a treasure that he wants you to use. Don't be afraid. He is not forceful, and we do not go forward in our own strength—push, push, pushing to the front. Instead, the Spirit gently stretches and grows you, knowing the right timing and the right order. But he also won't allow you to hide behind high chairs and laundry piles. Daughter, you are called, right where you are, to use your gifting—in your home, in your church, in the world.

DECLARE OUT LOUD OVER YOURSELF

I have been entrusted with a precious gift, and I will not let it go to waste or hide it away. I will use it for his Kingdom.

DECLARE OUT LOUD OVER YOUR CHILD

[Child's name] has been entrusted with a precious gift, and they will not let it go to waste or hide it away. They will use it for his Kingdom.

CONNECT WITH YOUR HEAVENLY FATHER

What is one (or more) thing(s) you're thankful for? What is something you appreciate about who God is? Set a timer for one minute. Wherever you are, pause and rest in his presence.

78

YOU ARE . . .
THE START OF SOMETHING NEW

Forget the former things; do not dwell on the

past. See, I am doing a new thing! Now it springs

up; do you not perceive it? I am making a way in

the wilderness and streams in the wasteland.

ISAIAH 43:18-19, NIV

(If you have more time: Isaiah 43:10-21.)

You are not who you came from or what you've done. Generational curses and prior failures do not define you. Even good things that you have experienced or inherited are nothing compared to what God has for you now. Don't hope for what you have hoped for, or dream for what you have dreamed for in the past. We cannot receive new things if our hearts are full of the old. Replaying the past in our minds stops us from dreaming with our Father about the future. Sister-friend, he wants to create something new within us.

DECLARE OUT LOUD OVER YOURSELF
I am the start of something new.

DECLARE OUT LOUD OVER YOUR CHILD
[Child's name] is the start of something new.

CONNECT WITH YOUR HEAVENLY FATHER
What is one (or more) thing(s) you're thankful for? What is something you appreciate about who God is? Set a timer for one minute. Wherever you are, pause and rest in his presence.

79

YOU ARE . . .
DREAMING THE
DREAMS OF GOD

Take delight in the LORD,

and he will give you your heart's desires.

PSALM 37:4

(If you have more time: Psalm 37:3-23.)

Daughter, when your heart is right, you can begin to hear the Lord through the desires he gives you. Our hopes and dreams are some of the ways that he wants to transform this world and bring about his Kingdom. When we give our longings to him, he may take our gift—our "loaves and fishes"—and multiply it to feed thousands or keep it as an intimate meal that brings joy and fullness to only a few. But no dream of God is silly; no mission from him is too insignificant; no sacrifice to him is a waste. Your heart's desire may just be an echo of his.

DECLARE OUT LOUD OVER YOURSELF

The Lord will fulfill the desires that he has put in my heart.

DECLARE OUT LOUD OVER YOUR CHILD

The Lord will fulfill the desires that he has put in [child's name]'s heart.

CONNECT WITH YOUR HEAVENLY FATHER

What is one (or more) thing(s) you're thankful for? What is something you appreciate about who God is? Set a timer for one minute. Wherever you are, pause and rest in his presence.

80

YOU ARE . . .
MADE FOR ETERNITY

He has made everything beautiful *and* appropriate in

its time. He has also planted eternity [a sense of divine

purpose] in the human heart [a mysterious longing which

nothing under the sun can satisfy, except God]—yet man

cannot find out (comprehend, grasp) what God has done

(His overall plan) from the beginning to the end.

ECCLESIASTES 3:11, AMP

(If you have more time: Ecclesiastes 3:1-15.)

The longing in your heart is God-birthed and can only be God-fulfilled. You are meant to be dissatisfied with what this world offers. Daughter, don't despise the dreams and desires of your heart or the part of you that says, *I was made for more.* Bring that sense of eternity to your Father and talk with him about it. Your yearnings—whether for sourdough or speaking, crocheting or coding, homeschooling or health care, or anything in between—might be his. When we dream with our Father, the world changes.

DECLARE OUT LOUD OVER YOURSELF

God has planted eternity in my heart; my longings are answered by his divine purpose and plan.

DECLARE OUT LOUD OVER YOUR CHILD

God has planted eternity in [child's name]'s heart; their longings are answered by his divine purpose and plan.

CONNECT WITH YOUR HEAVENLY FATHER

What is one (or more) thing(s) you're thankful for? What is something you appreciate about who God is? Set a timer for one minute. Wherever you are, pause and rest in his presence.

81

YOU ARE . . .
GOD'S MOUTHPIECE

Then the LORD reached out and touched my mouth and said, "Look, I have put my words in your mouth! Today I appoint you to stand up against nations and kingdoms. Some you must uproot and tear down, destroy and overthrow. Others you must build up and plant."

JEREMIAH 1:9-10
(If you have more time: Jeremiah 1:1-10.)

Sister-friend, what you say is powerful. God's words are even more powerful. With our words, we can heal and build, or we can tear down and destroy. God has given our words weight, and his words in our mouths have been given an assignment (see Isaiah 55:11). What we say can impact the direction of our loved ones and our nations. We can build his Kingdom and cause his will to be done, or bring destruction to strongholds and powers. Daughter, you are the mouthpiece of God on earth.

DECLARE OUT LOUD OVER YOURSELF

God's words in my mouth plant heaven's rule here on earth.

DECLARE OUT LOUD OVER YOUR CHILD

God's words in [child's name]'s mouth plant heaven's rule here on earth.

CONNECT WITH YOUR HEAVENLY FATHER

What is one (or more) thing(s) you're thankful for? What is something you appreciate about who God is? Set a timer for one minute. Wherever you are, pause and rest in his presence.

82

YOU ARE . . .
GIVEN HIS DIVINE NATURE

Because of his glory and excellence,

he has given us great and precious promises.

These are the promises that enable you to

share his divine nature and escape the

world's corruption caused by human desires.

2 PETER 1:4

(If you have more time. 2 Peter 1:3-11.)

Daughter, your destiny is to share in God's very nature and overcoming power. His promises are more than just words—they are the proof and the access to everything he has for us. When you were added to his family, you were removed from sin's control and corruption. His Spirit, his Word, and his nature have been implanted within you and are at work transforming everything—your life, your desires, and even this world.

DECLARE OUT LOUD OVER YOURSELF

The divine nature and promises given to me by God overcome this world.

DECLARE OUT LOUD OVER YOUR CHILD

The divine nature and promises given to [child's name] by God overcome this world.

CONNECT WITH YOUR HEAVENLY FATHER

What is one (or more) thing(s) you're thankful for? What is something you appreciate about who God is? Set a timer for one minute. Wherever you are, pause and rest in his presence.

83

YOU ARE . . .
AN OVERCOMER

You, dear children, are from God and have

overcome them, because the one who is in you

is greater than the one who is in the world.

1 JOHN 4:4, NIV

(If you have more time: 1 John 4:1-6.)

Daughter, you are called an overcomer so many times in the Word. There is nothing that can take you out or claim victory over you, because the Victor—who is over all powers and principalities, all rulers and dominions, and all created things—is with you. His Spirit resides within you. He will fight for you, give you strategy, share his power, and even enable you to do what you cannot do on your own. Because there is nothing that can defeat him, there is nothing that can defeat you.

DECLARE OUT LOUD OVER YOURSELF

I will overcome—because the One who is in me is greater than the one who is in the world..

DECLARE OUT LOUD OVER YOUR CHILD

[Child's name] will overcome—because the One who is in them is greater than the one who is in the world.

CONNECT WITH YOUR HEAVENLY FATHER

What is one (or more) thing(s) you're thankful for? What is something you appreciate about who God is? Set a timer for one minute. Wherever you are, pause and rest in his presence.

Because there is nothing
that can defeat him, there is
nothing that can defeat you.

84

YOU ARE . . .
CREATED TO RULE

Then God blessed them and said, "Be fruitful

and multiply. Fill the earth and govern it. Reign

over the fish in the sea, the birds in the sky, and

all the animals that scurry along the ground."

GENESIS 1:28

(If you have more time: Genesis 1:26–2:4.)

Daughter of the King, you were created to be the ruler of this earth and everything in it. God has given you his authority and made you his heir. You are not a bystander to your life or the happenings of this world. A charge and a purpose were given to man and woman at Creation. We are the rightful governors. The enemy wants our position. But he is a faker, a usurper, and a fraudulent ruler who has stolen your birthright. Daughter, you have been given everything you need to rule and reign as God's delegate on this earth.

DECLARE OUT LOUD OVER YOURSELF

I will carry out God's rule and reign on this earth.

DECLARE OUT LOUD OVER YOUR CHILD

[Child's name] will carry out God's rule and reign on this earth.

CONNECT WITH YOUR HEAVENLY FATHER

What is one (or more) thing(s) you're thankful for? What is something you appreciate about who God is? Set a timer for one minute. Wherever you are, pause and rest in his presence.

85

YOU ARE . . .
HOLDING THE KEYS

I will give you the keys of the kingdom of heaven.

Whatever you imprison, God will imprison. And

whatever you set free, God will set free.

MATTHEW 16:19, GW

(If you have more time: Matthew 16:13-20.)

God's plan for you to govern this earth has not changed. As we were charged in Eden, so we are charged now. We have been entrusted with the keys and the authority to bring everything under God's rule. He gave us control over what happens here; he backs our decrees. Mama, the places and situations you are in are not an accident. With his help and direction, we can bring God's order and blessings to our hearts, our homes, and our world.

DECLARE OUT LOUD OVER YOURSELF

God desires and enables me to bring his order and blessings to my heart, my home, and this earth.

DECLARE OUT LOUD OVER YOUR CHILD

God desires and enables [child's name] to bring his order and blessings to their heart, their home, and this earth.

CONNECT WITH YOUR HEAVENLY FATHER

What is one (or more) thing(s) you're thankful for? What is something you appreciate about who God is? Set a timer for one minute. Wherever you are, pause and rest in his presence.

86

YOU ARE . . . DESIGNED TO FULFILL GOD'S PLAN

The created world itself can hardly wait for what's coming next. Everything in creation is being more or less held back. God reins it in until both creation and all the creatures are ready and can be released at the same moment into the glorious times ahead. Meanwhile, the joyful anticipation deepens.

ROMANS 8:19-21, MSG

(If you have more time: Romans 8:18-30.)

Holy Daughter, you have a role to play in creation's freedom and God's reign here on earth. In his Kingdom, there is a place you were designed to fill. Where does the longing of your heart lead you to? Is it to home, to a hospital, to a classroom, to a courtroom, to something much more than you could even imagine? If your heart is yielded to and set on him, it may be the Spirit's longing that is directing you. Ask him. Ask your Father about his heart for you. All of creation is waiting for you to fulfill your part in bringing his rule and order.

DECLARE OUT LOUD OVER YOURSELF

I am a necessary part in fulfilling God's plan for all of creation.

DECLARE OUT LOUD OVER YOUR CHILD

[Child's name] is a necessary part in fulfilling God's plan for all of creation.

CONNECT WITH YOUR HEAVENLY FATHER

What is one (or more) thing(s) you're thankful for? What is something you appreciate about who God is? Set a timer for one minute. Wherever you are, pause and rest in his presence.

87

YOU ARE . . .
NEEDED

He makes the whole body fit together perfectly.

As each part does its own special work, it helps

the other parts grow, so that the whole body is

healthy and growing and full of love.

EPHESIANS 4:16

(If you have more time: Ephesians 4:11-16.)

Daughter, there are children of God who are waiting for your yes. We are interdependent. Our growth, healing, and victories are intertwined. Consider Joshua and Caleb who had to wait forty years to take the Promised Land because of others' disobedience. Your family and your local body need you and your unique contributions in order to flourish. It is not selfish for you to be who God has called you to be; it is selfish not to.

DECLARE OUT LOUD OVER YOURSELF

I will help others by doing the work God has made me for.

DECLARE OUT LOUD OVER YOUR CHILD

[Child's name] will help others by doing the work God has made them for.

CONNECT WITH YOUR HEAVENLY FATHER

What is one (or more) thing(s) you're thankful for? What is something you appreciate about who God is? Set a timer for one minute. Wherever you are, pause and rest in his presence.

I PRESS ON

TO TAKE HOLD
OF THAT FOR
WHICH CHRIST
JESUS TOOK
HOLD OF ME.

PHILIPPIANS 3:12, NIV

88

YOU ARE . . .
HERE FOR A REASON

Not that I have already obtained all this,

or have already arrived at my goal,

but I press on to take hold of that for

which Christ Jesus took hold of me.

PHILIPPIANS 3:12, NIV

(If you have more time: Philippians 3:1-12.)

Sister-friend, we have been purchased with the blood of Jesus Christ for a reason. The Spirit of God with his unlimited power lives within us. We have been offered every resource of heaven to aid us. Almighty God has not done and given all this so we can sit back and live a comfortable life. Let us seek and press in to attain all that he has for us. We will not be satisfied and the Kingdom will not be whole until we do.

DECLARE OUT LOUD OVER YOURSELF

I will press in to attain what God has for me.

DECLARE OUT LOUD OVER YOUR CHILD

[Child's name] will press in to attain what God has for them.

CONNECT WITH YOUR HEAVENLY FATHER

What is one (or more) thing(s) you're thankful for? What is something you appreciate about who God is? Set a timer for one minute. Wherever you are, pause and rest in his presence.

89

YOU ARE . . .
ON A MISSION

In the same way that you gave me [Jesus]

a mission in the world, I give them

a mission in the world.

JOHN 17:18, MSG

(If you have more time: John 17:6-21.)

Mama, you have been specifically chosen, handpicked by God in love. You do not just happen to be here in this moment of eternity. It is not just by chance that you are a mother to your individual child or children. There is nothing random about how you were created. God determined long ago that you would be his. And he gave you a mission for which you are divinely prepared and fashioned. Don't just get by; seek out what he has prepared for you. You matter more than you know.

DECLARE OUT LOUD OVER YOURSELF

You have given me a mission in this world, and I will accomplish it.

DECLARE OUT LOUD OVER YOUR CHILD

You have given [child's name] a mission in this world, and they will accomplish it.

CONNECT WITH YOUR HEAVENLY FATHER

What is one (or more) thing(s) you're thankful for? What is something you appreciate about who God is? Set a timer for one minute. Wherever you are, pause and rest in his presence.

90

YOU ARE . . .
BEING PREPARED FOR
GREATER THINGS

Your servant has killed both the lion and the

bear; and this uncircumcised Philistine will

be like one of them, since he has taunted

and defied the armies of the living God.

I SAMUEL 17:36, AMP

(If you have more time: 1 Samuel 17:32-50.)

Mama, don't let the lion and the bear take you down. These enemies and challenges are not meant to defeat you; they will not always stand against you. In David's life, every battle and victory prepared him for the next one. The same is true for you. Don't be discouraged by the things you are walking through now, and don't despise the insignificance of everyday battles and victories. Like David's did, they are enlarging God's Kingdom, freeing and encouraging his children, and preparing you for what comes next.

DECLARE OUT LOUD OVER YOURSELF

Victories over the lions, bears, and giants in my life are coming and are preparing me for God's purpose.

DECLARE OUT LOUD OVER YOUR CHILD

Victories over the lions, bears, and giants in [child's name]'s life are coming and are preparing them for God's purpose.

CONNECT WITH YOUR HEAVENLY FATHER

What is one (or more) thing(s) you're thankful for? What is something you appreciate about who God is? Set a timer for one minute. Wherever you are, pause and rest in his presence.

91

YOU ARE . . .
NOT FORGOTTEN

The Lord will work out his plans for my life—

for your loving-kindness, Lord, continues

forever. Don't abandon me—for you made me.

PSALM 138:8, TLB

(If you have more time: Psalm 138:1-8.)

Daughter, there is no need to worry or strive or manipulate to ensure that the Lord's purpose for you and your family will come to pass. No one can stop what he has planned. No thing can stand in the way. It doesn't matter who is or isn't on your side or following you on Instagram. He will not give up on you or your purpose. His love is not dependent on you or what you have done. It stretches from eternity to eternity, without pause and without end. You are his, and he will not abandon you or what he has planned for your life.

DECLARE OUT LOUD OVER YOURSELF

There is no man or woman, no power or principality, no situation or authority that can stand in the way of what God has said concerning me.

DECLARE OUT LOUD OVER YOUR CHILD

There is no man or woman, no power or principality, no situation or authority that can stand in the way of what God has said concerning [child's name].

CONNECT WITH YOUR HEAVENLY FATHER

What is one (or more) thing(s) you're thankful for? What is something you appreciate about who God is? Set a timer for one minute. Wherever you are, pause and rest in his presence.

92

YOU ARE . . .
MADE FOR MORE

Make your tent bigger; stretch it out and make

it wider. Do not hold back. Make the ropes

longer and its stakes stronger, because you

will spread out to the right and to the left. Your

children will take over other nations, and they

will again live in cities that once were destroyed.

ISAIAH 54:2-3, NCV

(If you have more time: Isaiah 54:1-17.)

Mama, your Father does not want to restrict you; he wants you to grow. When the time is right, you will not be able to contain all that the Lord has for you. You are not meant to live a small, stale life. Wherever the Lord has planted you, he will increase you. His Word whispers to your heart, "I have so much more for you." Secure yourself deep and firmly in him; dare to hope again.

DECLARE OUT LOUD OVER YOURSELF

I will not hold back my hope, because God has more for me.

DECLARE OUT LOUD OVER YOUR CHILD

[Child's name] will not hold back their hope, because God has more for them.

CONNECT WITH YOUR HEAVENLY FATHER

What is one (or more) thing(s) you're thankful for? What is something you appreciate about who God is? Set a timer for one minute. Wherever you are, pause and rest in his presence.

93

YOU ARE . . .
ANSWERED WITH YES

You can ask for anything in my name,

and I will do it, so that the Son can bring glory

to the Father. Yes, ask me for anything

in my name, and I will do it!

JOHN 14:13-14

(If you have more time: John 14:1-14.)

Daughter, it brings your Father God glory to say yes to the requests you ask in Jesus' name. Jesus instructs us to ask him. It is not selfish to pray for success in what he has called you to do. Our victories enlarge his glory and his fame. In a dark world, he wants your ability, your influence, and your light to increase. What you accomplish—especially when it is beyond what you could do or know on your own—testifies to his power and excellence. The world will know his goodness through your life. So, Sister-friend, ask him; he is waiting to say yes.

DECLARE OUT LOUD OVER YOURSELF

God will say yes to his plans for me for his glory's sake.

DECLARE OUT LOUD OVER YOUR CHILD

God will say yes to his plans for [child's name] for his glory's sake.

CONNECT WITH YOUR HEAVENLY FATHER

What is one (or more) thing(s) you're thankful for? What is something you appreciate about who God is? Set a timer for one minute. Wherever you are, pause and rest in his presence.

94

YOU ARE . . .
BLESSED IN YOUR WORK

The LORD will open the heavens, the storehouse

of his bounty, to send rain on your land in season

and to bless all the work of your hands. You will

lend to many nations but will borrow from none.

DEUTERONOMY 28:12, NIV

(If you have more time: Deuteronomy 28:1-14.)

When we are working in step with God, he promises to bless the work we are doing. His desire is for us to be successful. His covenant is that he will give us his divine favor and excellence in whatever we do. This includes motherhood, business, ministry, and more. He will match our hard work with his resources. His storehouse is opened to give us all that we need. With him, there is no lack. Our success brings him glory.

DECLARE OUT LOUD OVER YOURSELF

The Lord will bless the work I do.

DECLARE OUT LOUD OVER YOUR CHILD

The Lord will bless the work [child's name] does.

CONNECT WITH YOUR HEAVENLY FATHER

What is one (or more) thing(s) you're thankful for? What is something you appreciate about who God is? Set a timer for one minute. Wherever you are, pause and rest in his presence.

God's plan is for you to
succeed and overcome.

95

YOU ARE . . .
A TESTAMENT

Then their offspring will be known among the
nations, and their descendants among the
peoples. All who see them [in their prosperity]
will recognize *and* acknowledge them that they
are the people whom the Lord has blessed.

ISAIAH 61:9, AMP

(If you have more time: Isaiah 61:1-11.)

Dearest one, God is represented by us, his people. He desires for his name and character to be known throughout the world. This does not mean that you will never struggle or experience hard things, but it does mean that his plan is for you to succeed and overcome. Paul was imprisoned, but even in his hardship, he excelled and accomplished his mission to spread the gospel. Know and believe that God is glorified by blessing you. When you prosper, you are a testament to his faithfulness, his excellence, and his overcoming power.

DECLARE OUT LOUD OVER YOURSELF

God will cause my life to be a picture of his excellence and power.

DECLARE OUT LOUD OVER YOUR CHILD

God will cause [child's name]'s life to be a picture of his excellence and power.

CONNECT WITH YOUR HEAVENLY FATHER

What is one (or more) thing(s) you're thankful for? What is something you appreciate about who God is? Set a timer for one minute. Wherever you are, pause and rest in his presence.

96

YOU ARE . . .
HIS LIGHT IN THE WORLD

You are the light that gives light to the world.

A city that is built on a hill cannot be hidden.

MATTHEW 5:14, ICB

(If you have more time: Matthew 5:1-16.)

Daughter, God gave you the job of bringing light—his rule and all that comes with it—into the world. Jesus was, among other things, our example: He brought life, joy, peace, and order wherever he went; he transformed everything he touched. The Holy Spirit's presence is in you, and you bring him into every situation and place you are in. What you do and say brings God's light to the places and people who are in the dark, even when it doesn't feel like it. Never underestimate what your light can do.

DECLARE OUT LOUD OVER YOURSELF

I am his light to this world and the people in it.

DECLARE OUT LOUD OVER YOUR CHILD

[Child's name] is his light to this world and the people in it.

CONNECT WITH YOUR HEAVENLY FATHER

What is one (or more) thing(s) you're thankful for? What is something you appreciate about who God is? Set a timer for one minute. Wherever you are, pause and rest in his presence.

97

YOU ARE . . .
EVIDENCE OF
SIGNS AND WONDERS

Here am I and the children whom the

LORD has given me! We are for signs and

wonders in Israel from the LORD of hosts,

who dwells in Mount Zion.

ISAIAH 8:18, NKJV

(If you have more time: Isaiah 8:11-18.)

Mama, you are a sign of God to this generation. His goodness and his ways, his justice and his truth will be displayed through you. He has chosen you to be a picture of him. Your peace assures this world of his strength. When others tremble, your joy shows his faithfulness. The righteousness of Christ within you shows the way of truth. Your abundance shows his provision. Your life is to be so much more than anything you could do or explain on your own.

DECLARE OUT LOUD OVER YOURSELF

I am for signs and wonders.

DECLARE OUT LOUD OVER YOUR CHILD

[Child's name] is for signs and wonders.

CONNECT WITH YOUR HEAVENLY FATHER

What is one (or more) thing(s) you're thankful for? What is something you appreciate about who God is? Set a timer for one minute. Wherever you are, pause and rest in his presence.

98

YOU ARE . . .
A BLESSING

I will make you into a great nation. I will bless you
and make you famous, and you will be a blessing to
others. I will bless those who bless you and curse
those who treat you with contempt. All the families
on earth will be blessed through you.

GENESIS 12:2-3

(If you have more time: Genesis 12:1-7 and Galatians 3:14.)

Precious Mama, there is a reason you feel like you were made for more. And I don't mean that what you're doing isn't big enough. I mean that changing diapers is not just changing diapers, and doing laundry is about more than keeping your family in clean clothes. Writing a book is about more than typing words. Our tasks are not our calling. Whether your days are filled with diapers, lesson plans, patient charting, or anything in between, each act is part of a larger purpose. You are called to change hearts, renew minds, touch lives, and bring about his Kingdom. God's covenant to bless all the families of the earth through his people is carried on in you.

DECLARE OUT LOUD OVER YOURSELF

I am a blessing to this earth.

DECLARE OUT LOUD OVER YOUR CHILD

[Child's name] is a blessing to this earth.

CONNECT WITH YOUR HEAVENLY FATHER

What is one (or more) thing(s) you're thankful for? What is something you appreciate about who God is? Set a timer for one minute. Wherever you are, pause and rest in his presence.

99

YOU ARE . . .
NOT BEING EXTINGUISHED

For this reason I remind you to kindle afresh the
gift of God which is in you through the laying on
of my hands. For God has not given us a spirit of
timidity, but of power and love and discipline.

2 TIMOTHY 1:6-7, NASB

(If you have more time: 2 Timothy 1:5-14.)

Daughter, motherhood is not the end of your purpose. It is not meant to be a place to bury your gifts. Your heavenly Father calls you to kindle afresh what he has placed in you. This time may not be a loud or active season for practicing your giftings, but it is also not meant to put out your flame. It may be a time of deepening your relationship with God and disciplining your heart and character. Even when it looks different than you think, you are encouraged not to shrink back. Instead, through his power, love, and discipline, nurture what you have been given.

DECLARE OUT LOUD OVER YOURSELF

God has not forgotten the gift he gave me, and I will not be timid in accepting his call.

DECLARE OUT LOUD OVER YOUR CHILD

God has not forgotten the gift he gave [child's name], and they will not be timid in accepting his call.

CONNECT WITH YOUR HEAVENLY FATHER

What is one (or more) thing(s) you're thankful for? What is something you appreciate about who God is? Set a timer for one minute. Wherever you are, pause and rest in his presence.

100

YOU ARE . . . SUMMONED

Who has done such mighty deeds, summoning each new generation from the beginning of time? It is I, the LORD, the First and the Last. I alone am he.

ISAIAH 41:4

(If you have more time: Isaiah 41:1-10.)

Out of all eras and locations, God chose you for exactly when and where you are. You are meant to impact eternity by fulfilling your role in this moment. In him, our temporary existence becomes something eternal. God from everlasting to everlasting has determined and designed time and space to meet in your life right now, for his purposes. Daughter, you have been summoned forth from the beginning of time and given a mission. How could you not answer the call?

DECLARE OUT LOUD OVER YOURSELF

The Lord has summoned me forth from eternity for this time, right now, and I will answer his call.

DECLARE OUT LOUD OVER YOUR CHILD

The Lord has summoned [child's name] forth from eternity for this time, right now, and they will answer his call.

CONNECT WITH YOUR HEAVENLY FATHER

What is one (or more) thing(s) you're thankful for? What is something you appreciate about who God is? Set a timer for one minute. Wherever you are, pause and rest in his presence.

HE IS OVERWHELMED BY **YOUR OFFERING.**

FAREWELL FOR NOW

I STARTED WRITING THIS BOOK after a back porch conversation with my two friends. But God started writing it in me much earlier. I have already shared some of what I went through with my baby girl's self-soothing delay. But I did not share how deeply exhausted I was. For months, I was fortunate if she slept an hour or two (nonconsecutively) every night—I don't know how either of us survived it. In so many areas, I was scraping bottom only for my bloodied fingers to come up lacking.

Still, almost every morning I would peel myself out from under the blankets, pick up my daughter who had just finished nursing beside me, and head to the dimly lit kitchen in our trailer. I set her bouncer on the table right beside my Bible, left the lights low, and hoped everyone would stay settled for just a few more moments.

Even though I was so tired in my body and mind, I was desperate to see my Savior's face, to make eye contact with my Father. I needed to feel his embrace, to melt into him and allow his love and peace to melt into me . . . and once settled, to join my words with his Words in a holy "Amen," defiantly gripping and holding up once again the Sword of the Spirit over myself and my family.

And just as with the widow at the Temple, he was overwhelmed by my offering.

Your life's details are most likely different from mine, but the heart of your story is the same. Even with everything you have been through and everything you are going through now, you have made the time to come. The holy moments you have spent here are an exquisite and priceless gift. Your Father receives it with open arms, knowing that you have given all that you have and maybe even what you didn't. And, Sister-friend, he is overwhelmed by your offering.

Father God, you are worthy. You are worth all that we have given. May your love drench your daughters right now. May they feel and hear you rejoicing over them with joy, renewing them with your love, and exulting over them with singing (Zephaniah 3:17). Give them faith and the completion of all they have spoken before you. I agree and say, "Amen," that your Word will not return void in their lives or the lives of their families (Isaiah 55:11). Lord, bring them into your presence and into your arms. In the precious and powerful name of your Son and our Brother, Jesus, I ask and believe all these things. Hallelujah and amen.

ACKNOWLEDGMENTS

HOW CAN I POSSIBLY THANK EVERYONE who has contributed in some way to my life and therefore this book? If you have ever whispered a prayer on my behalf, shared a smile with me at the grocery store, or left a positive review; if you have ever made my hard times harder, questioned my motives, or spoken wrongly about me—if there has ever been a way we crossed paths, "Thank you." Our lives are a beautiful tapestry, dark colors and light, woven together throughout eternity by a God who lives in community. I am grateful for my life and the role you have played in it. By affecting me, you have affected all who read this book.

To My First and My Last, My Beginning and My End, the One who has always been there and has always been enough: Words cannot describe the gratitude and love I have for you. You are my rear guard, my shoulder to cry on, my ever-present love, my Father, my Brother. There is no me that I want to be without you. If I lost everything but you, I would still find peace and joy in your arms.

To Mom and Dad and all the rest of my crazy Copple family: It wasn't pretty, but we're still standing. You built our house upon the Rock, and though the storms and winds tore things apart, our foundation held firm. Our family held to and was held by the One who "holds everything together" (Colossians 1:17, GW). Thank you for a million

different memories and for the family text chains that always make me laugh. I love you all.

To Mom and Dad and all the rest of my Assell family: Thank you for letting me in. I have never felt like an in-law or a secondary sister or daughter. When we were broken, your home is where we were put back together. God met me in your basement, and I believe it's because you welcomed him there long before we moved in. Thank you.

To Dave and Laura: You are lumped in with the family thank-yous because that is what you have been. Your prayers and counsel have shaped and refined me and my family. I appreciate your hard advice, your loving embraces, the shoulders I have cried on, and the stairs I have painted with you. You have kept us out of more trouble and saved us from more messes than I probably know. We would be a disaster without you. May you experience the joy of seeing us, your spiritual children, walk in truth, and the fruit of all your hard labor for us.

To our church body: You have upheld this book and so many others in prayer. You have prayed us through hard times and through victory. When we wept, you wept. When we celebrated, you celebrated. I cannot count the number of prayers, meals, encouragements, cards, and hugs you have given to me and my family. You have truly been the arms, hands, and body of Christ to us.

To my PBC girls: You are what movies are made of. When I was young, I dreamed of having friends like you someday. Your support and love seem too extravagant. "Thank you" seems too small to capture how deeply grateful I am to you for cheering me on, buying books the moment the presale was available, buying the plane tickets, kidnapping me for my birthday, pre-reading most of this book through my texts and questions to you, adding to the Pinterest design board and helping me pick title names, listening when I ranted and cried and laughed—for praying, praying, praying. I am SOOOOO grateful for you. I hope I love you half as well as you love me.

To the Tyndale Team: Thank you. Sharon, thank you for hearing the Holy Spirit; I hope you get to see all the lives our Father touches through this. Jillian, thank you for your never-ending support and encouragement. You steered this all the way through. Bonne, I learned so much from you. Thank you for your patience and willingness to let me keep fiddling with it all. Dean and Julie, thank you for making this book beautiful. Kaylee, it was so wonderful knowing you were on my team and advocating for me and this book. Linda (on the children's book team), thank you for believing in me so many years ago. Look what God has done! To the copy editors and the proofreaders, to the marketing and sales teams—thank you. I know I'm missing so many more. Forgive me and know that God will take the seeds you have planted for his Kingdom and grow them into so much more than you could have ever imagined.

Gabe (I know you're already rolling your eyes as you read this, but I'm documenting it for all time anyway): You were the reason we wanted to change in the first place. You were my motivation to get up and try again, to be better than I ever thought I could be. You might be our only child who remembers the early, hard days of our family, but I can see how God has used it for good in your life and your future. You will change the world. I can't believe God chose me to be your mom. It is the greatest honor of my life. Sorry you had to do so many dishes and eat so many frozen pizzas while I was writing this book.

Natalie Darling: I want to be like you when I grow up. You have fiercely overcome more than most adults ever will. When things became hard, you turned toward love instead of turning away or turning to bitterness. Your vulnerability and soft heart are so beautiful. The love you have for God is second only to how much love he has for you. Thank you for bringing me endless cans of LaCroix and coffee refills. I hope this book is a reminder for you to dream and live the dreams God has for you.

LoLo, my firecracker, the one who can always make me smile, my child raised in freedom: "I love your face." You are light. Thank you for teaching me more about God and about being a beloved child than I could have ever known on my own. When I need to understand how and how much God loves me, I only have to think of how much I adore you. Thank you for cuddling with me and believing in me.

Matt: The only person who believes in me and has fought for me as much as you is our heavenly Father. You are my rock. You pulled me back up on my feet more times than I can count. You wouldn't let me give up or stay silent. You have seen me fail, and then unconditionally and courageously told me that's not who I am. You have spoken truth when I didn't want to hear it, and listened to waaay more words than you ever wanted to. It's been messy. It's been raw. It's been beautiful. I'm so glad it was you and not anyone else. You're my favorite.

ABOUT THE AUTHOR

EMILY ASSELL is a bestselling children's book author and speaker. She believes dry shampoo, snacks, and the Word of God can solve almost any parenting problem. She and her husband, Matt, started Generation Claimed in 2017 to self-publish her first book, *You Are*. A year later, Tyndale House Publishers released the book, which has gone on to sell over twenty-five thousand copies. When not writing, Emily homeschools her three children, volunteers at LoveMoves.Us (a nonprofit for foster and adoptive children and families), or gets lost reading someone else's book. Emily has spoken at many parenting conferences, schools, mothers' groups, and special events, and she has been a featured guest on multiple podcasts, teaching and encouraging all ages about the power of God's Word. But don't worry, her three kids are her own personal slang dictionary and keep her down-to-earth despite her best efforts to be cool.

Also by
Emily Assell

Available wherever books are sold.